BLACK MUSIC,
WHITE BUSINESS

BLACK MUSIC, WHITE BUSINESS

Illuminating the History and
Political Economy of Jazz

by Frank Kofsky

PATHFINDER

New York   London   Montreal   Sydney

ISBN 978-0-87348-859-4
Library of Congress Catalog Card Number 97-69547
Manufactured in the United States of America

Cover design: Susan Zárate
Front cover photograph: Charlie Parker/*Corbis-Bettman*

First edition, 1998
Sixth printing, 2010

Pathfinder
www.pathfinderpress.com
E-mail: pathfinder@pathfinderpress.com

To esther . . .

Who has always been proud of her nephew, regardless

Contents

Preface and
acknowledgements

This book is one of two companion volumes; it enters the world simultaneously with its sibling, *John Coltrane and the Jazz Revolution of the 1960s*, which is, in turn, the second and revised edition of *Black Nationalism and the Revolution in Music*.

To explain more fully, *Black Music, White Business* had its inception in my decision to undertake a new edition of *Black Nationalism and the Revolution in Music*, which (as I relate at greater length in the preface to *John Coltrane and the Jazz Revolution*) is something I had long wanted to do. After considerable thought about what such a revised and expanded book should include, I resolved to attempt a treatment of the history and political economy of jazz that would go beyond the scattered and not-entirely-systematic observations on these topics in the original. As the revising progressed, however, it gradually dawned on me that the new material had sufficiently important implications, and was sufficiently capable of standing independently, to merit a book in its own right. What is more, although there are ample connections between the main themes of the older work and the new ones I now wanted to discuss—anyone seeking to understand why jazz musicians are attracted to black nationalist ideology, for example, hardly need look beyond the first four chapters here—I began to suspect that I could not give those connections the emphasis they deserve without a great deal of repetitiousness. And, finally, because both the quality of my scholarship and my handling of certain musical questions had improved in the interval between the publication of *Black Nationalism* and its successor—or so, at any rate, I would like to believe—I was already finding it difficult, even without the additional chapters I envisioned, to hold the latter to a manageable length.

Taking all these considerations into account, I was compelled to conclude, albeit reluctantly, that my ideas might be easier for readers to digest if presented in the form of two related books, rather than stuffed willy-nilly between a single set of covers. Accordingly, what I had initially conceived of as the second edition of *Black Nationalism and the Revolution in Music* emerged at the end of a period of gestation as a pair of fraternal twins: identical in their parentage and hour of birth, but rather different in their physical and intellectual characteristics. One of these twins you now hold in your hands.

✳

Among the most enjoyable aspects of completing a book is the opportunity it affords an author to acknowledge all those whose assistance enabled him to bring the work to fruition.

It was my good fortune to be able to collaborate with Michael Baumann and his colleagues at Pathfinder Press, who went out of their way to make the sometimes-painful alchemy of transforming a manuscript into a book as pleasant as possible.

As is always the case when I write about jazz, Cliff and Julia Houdek stand high on the list of those to whom I am beholden; decades ago, they alerted me to the significance of young children's hand-clapping games for an understanding of why black and white youth arrive at maturity with different musical aptitudes and sensibilities. The essay in chapter 7 is my effort to build on their suggestions; the argument there also benefits from what I have learned from my students in the class in the History of Black Music in America at California State University, Sacramento, that I was at one time permitted to teach. More specifically, Les Pogue and Norman Harris brought the Hambone game to my attention, while Julie Blattler proffered new insights about the African roots of innovations in African-American music. I am also deeply grateful to Jane E. Light (then Jane Johnson), who proved ingenious and indefatigable in the research she did for me.

I owe a similarly large debt to two musician friends, drummer Jimmy Robinson of Sacramento and especially pianist-trombonist-composer Mark Levine of San Francisco. To say that chapters 2 and 3 would be immeasurably weaker if I had not been able to make use of the documents (reproduced in Appendices A and B) that Mark was so kind as to put in my hands is a gross understatement; the truth is that without the invaluable information he supplied, those chapters might not even exist.

Last, I certainly could not possibly publish a book on jazz without at some point voicing my thanks to all the artists who have shared in the creation of this unimaginably rich, moving and expressive music. This work, like everything else on the subject I have written, is part of my continuing effort to discharge what I regard as my moral obligation to them.

Frank Kofsky
BENICIA, CALIFORNIA
NOVEMBER 1996

Part 1

The political economy of jazz then and now

1

'You don't own your own product':
an introduction to
the political economy of jazz

Originally, I had not planned to bother with Nat Hentoff's book
Jazz Is,[1] but a casual acquaintance who had not read my own
book, *Black Nationalism and the Revolution in Music*,[2] wanted
to borrow a copy and suggested lending me the Hentoff volume in exchange.

I do believe the other party got the better of the transaction.

My initial reasons for choosing to avoid *Jazz Is* all have to
do with what in my eyes are the author's severe problems with
questions of ambivalence and identity. Specifically, Hentoff on
jazz never appears to be able to choose between, on the one hand,
attempting to impress his colleagues at *The New Yorker, Dis-
sent*, and *The Village Voice* with the magnitude of his vocabulary and (in that well-worn reviewer's phrase) "monumental
erudition" or, on the other, striking the tough-guy pose of the
writer who has absorbed his share of hard knocks in the course
of growing to young manhood in Boston's Jewish ghetto. Re-

lated but considerably more grave, Hentoff conveys the impression of someone in profound conflict over whether to be faithful to his professed socialist politics at the risk of alienating his friends and associates in the white business institutions of jazz, or whether to maintain these relationships even at the cost of biting his tongue. (As I bring out in later chapters, Hentoff is not the only white writer on jazz to face such a dilemma, but his work seems to reflect the tensions arising from it more acutely than any other.)

From reading him on and off over several decades, I have concluded that Hentoff has tried to resolve this second contradiction by invoking a wealth of radical-sounding phrases while in fact committing himself to nothing more than a collection of high-flown but completely abstract and vacuous generalizations (for instance, that the role of jazz in school curricula should be expanded).

In short, Hentoff comes across as an author who knows more—a good deal more—than he is willing to tell. At any time within the past forty years, for example, he could have carried out an investigation of the political economy of jazz far more readily than I: his involvement with the subject has been longer, the amount of material he has collected on it is certainly no less, and the availability of information to him through his ubiquitous connections with jazz-oriented businessmen can only be more extensive. And yet, I am positive that it would never seriously occur to Hentoff to undertake such a project, for to write on the political economy of jazz in a no-holds-barred fashion—not hesitating to mention names of individuals and corporations guilty of habitual abuse of jazz performers—would at once put him completely beyond the bounds of acceptability so far as the white businessmen who control the political economy of jazz are concerned.

Still, once a copy of Hentoff's book had fallen into my hands, curiosity led me to dip into a chapter here, another there. In this way, it did not take long to discover that this was just one more version of the usual compendium of thrown-together anecdotal material, neither much better nor much worse than one can find in any of a dozen books on jazz—a Jewish and ostentatiously "hip" effort, as it were, of the kind of square and quintessentially *goyishe* collection of essays assembled by Martin Williams under the title *The Jazz Tradition*[3] (and analyzed at length in chapter 6). Thus, there are the expected pieces on Duke Ellington, Miles Davis, John Coltrane, Cecil Taylor and—for some idiosyncratic reason I could not fathom and did not particularly care to ponder—one on the Argentinian saxophonist Gato Barbieri. Most of these miniatures are, heaven knows, innocuous enough—save for a pointlessly harsh and unempathetic treatment of Charlie Parker*—though an occasional morsel of interest did manage to insert itself into the text every so often.

Skipping about more or less randomly (*Jazz Is* has no table of contents to guide the reader), I came upon Hentoff's penul-

---

* See *Jazz Is*, pp. 173–95. I have always felt it the height of insensitivity for white writers—the bulk of whom have not for one moment left behind the safety of their safe harbor in the middle class—to indulge themselves in the luxury of sanctimonious moralizing at the expense of black musicians, especially when the accused, long since interred, are not even permitted the opportunity to present their side of the story. As a case in point, witness one white author condemn those who "have preferred to blame self-destructive life styles [of black musicians] on racism, poverty, crooked managers and the general social milieu rather than admit that a hero like Lester Young [or Charlie Parker] might simply have been weak in character" (John McDonough, "Books," *down beat*, November 2, 1978, p. 60). Such verdicts, the certain indicator of a petty-bourgeois mentality, are always "simply" dispensed when the judge has been sheltered by class and color from firsthand experience with the worst life has to offer. (To sample an entire volume of such condescension aimed at jazz artists, see Joe Goldberg, *Jazz Masters of the Fifties* [New York: Macmillan, 1965].)

What Nat Hentoff, like most whites who pronounce *ex cathedra* on black music and the lives of black musicians, fails to perceive is that the traits he criticizes so mindlessly in Parker would be celebrated (or at least tolerated) in a white artist, such as the poet Dylan Thomas, as outward manifestations of a gifted but tortured inner sensibility.

It is also germane that artistic precociousness is difficult enough to cope with even in the most stable surroundings—and Parker's were anything but that. At age fifteen, he left school to concentrate exclusively on his music. At that time if not before, he became immersed in the night life of Kansas City, in which temptations of every sort abounded. Talented to a near-superhuman degree, imma-

timate chapter, with the promising title, "The Political Economy of Jazz." That heading, as it turned out, was one of the only two assets to which this truncated essay (fewer than ten pages in length) can lay claim. The other is a quotation from trumpeter Rex Stewart that begins the chapter's fourth paragraph:

> Where the control is, the money is. Do you see any of us [black musicians] running any record companies, booking agencies, radio stations, music magazines?[4]

"Wonderful!" I thought to myself, "Maybe Hentoff is finally going to say something after all." But any such hopes were soon enough extinguished when I turned the page. Instead of following the crystal-clear lead suggested by Rex Stewart's remark, Hentoff could scarcely wait to be rid of such explosive topics as money, power, and business ownership in order to plunge instead into a predictably unenlightening and entirely superfluous discussion of the position of jazz in the nation's educational systems. Not only is this latter subject one of secondary importance at most in any analysis of the political economy of jazz, but it has already been examined for black colleges by LeRoi Jones and for white ones by myself.[5] So besides showing himself utterly unwilling to confront the ugly truths that a thoroughgoing investigation of the political economy of jazz would be sure to unearth, Hentoff apparently did not even have one original thought for his readers' consideration. As for Rex Stewart's comment—easily superior to anything else in the chapter—its function evidently is to provide a brief moment of titillation before the author rapidly scurries into less controversial waters where potentially embarrassing questions are unlikely to arise.

ture and wholly deprived of adult supervision, is it any wonder that Parker's personality development took the direction it did? Would yours, mine, or even Mr. Hentoff's be likely to fare better in similar circumstances? The premature deaths of white rock performers Janis Joplin, Brian Jones, Jim Morrison, and Keith Moon in the 1960s and 1970s suggest an answer in the negative.

＊

After finishing with Hentoff's pusillanimous treatment, I could not shake the conviction that an inquiry more concerned to reveal than to conceal the fundamental nature of the political economy of jazz would necessarily be compelled to explore such questions as alienation, underemployment, and racist contempt for black music; powerlessness and the qualitatively heightened exploitation of the black artist; the double standard for black versus white art music in the recording industry; ideological mystification in the jazz world; and so on. In the remaining pages of this introduction, I will merely sketch in broad strokes an outline of each of these aspects of the political economy of jazz, reserving a more complete discussion for the chapters that follow.

Alienation. The essence of the political economy of jazz has never been stated with greater succinctness than in saxophonist Archie Shepp's aphorism, "You own the music and we make it." Further clarification, should any be needed, comes from the comment of Rex Stewart I quoted earlier: "Where the control is, the money is. Do you see any of us running any record companies, booking agencies, radio stations, music magazines?"

The technical term for this phenomenon, in which the ultimate disposition of the fruits of a person's labor is in the hands of his employer, is *alienation*. In the classic nineteenth-century sense in which the word is still used today, alienation occurs because the employer and not the worker controls both the means of production (factories, machines, tools, and the like) and the products manufactured by human labor through the operation of these means. A jazz artist, of course, does own the tools of his trade, so to speak, but is nonetheless alienated from what he himself has created by the fact that he must depend on those who control the means of *distribution*—nightclubs, festivals, concerts, radio stations and, above all else, booking agencies and recording companies—in order to bring his music before the public to earn a livelihood from it.

Two consequences flow directly from this situation: (1) the artistry of the jazz musician operates primarily to enrich not its possessor, but those white executives who own and/or manage the means of production and distribution within the political economy of jazz; and (2) the decisions of such owners and managers, particularly those involved in the recording industry, are absolutely crucial in determining both the total amount of employment for black musicians and which specific musicians will be granted access to it (see chapter 4 for an extended treatment of this point).

Even though black musicians themselves do not ordinarily employ the term "alienation," one should not make the mistake of thinking that they are unaware of the phenomenon. Thus, saxophonist and composer Ornette Coleman told author A.B. Spellman that

> the problem in this business is that you don't own your own product. If you record, it's the record company that owns it; if you play at a club, it's the nightclub owners who charge people to listen to you, and then they tell you your music is not catching on. Let's say I've made eight albums; if one company owns six of them and the other owns two, then who do you think made the most money from them? Me or the two companies? . . .
>
> This has been my greatest problem—being shortchanged because I'm a Negro, not because I can't produce. Here I am being used as a Negro who can play jazz, and all the people I recorded for and worked for act as if they own me and my product. *They have been guilty of making me believe I shouldn't have the profits from my product simply because they own the channels of production* [my italics]. . . . They act like I owe them something for letting me express myself with my music, like the artist is supposed to suffer and not to live in clean, comfortable situations. . . .
>
> The insanity of living in America is that ownership is really strength. It's who owns who's strongest in America. . . . That's why it's so hard to lend your music to that kind of existence.[6]

Underemployment, contempt. The second most important fact to bear in mind is that, largely as a consequence of the alienated position of the jazz artist, un- and underemployment are chronic afflictions with which he must live and attempt to work (see chapters 3 and 4 for more on this subject). Which is to say that the persistent denial of a chance to earn a decent living comes about for jazz artists not primarily because of the prevailing conditions, but rather *because of the attitudes toward jazz and black music generally of the white executives who control the means of producing and distributing it.* To be sure, in some situations—such as a depression, when sales of recordings of all types decline—the executives will have their freedom of action curtailed by external restraints. But where jazz is concerned, they are essentially autonomous. They are able, in other words, to expand or contract the extent of their jazz operations almost at will, confident that the size of the public for jazz will in nearly all cases increase or decrease accordingly.

It follows, then, that how the white executives who dominate the processes of production and distribution of jazz regard that form of black music is of the utmost significance in determining the level of employment available to jazz artists at any given time. As I will illustrate extensively in chapter 3, the historical tendency has been for these executives to view jazz and jazz musicians with racist contempt—and, furthermore, this generalization can be shown to apply to some of the white executives who have been most successful in carving out lucrative careers for themselves in the field of jazz. As a consequence, therefore, even when such executives do choose to undertake a certain amount of activity in the sphere of jazz, the level of employment they create is still kept artificially and unnecessarily low by their scorn for black music and the artists who perform it.

Powerlessness and qualitatively heightened exploitation. It is a truism in labor history that the ability of workers to improve the conditions under which they toil is always least during periods of high unemployment. In jazz, such periods are the rule.

As a result, jazz musicians are perennially in the position of having to sell their creativity in a buyers' market, a state of affairs that, as they and the white executives who profit from their talents both are aware, drastically reduces their power to bargain for the kind of treatment that befits a serious musical artist.

If this relative powerlessness vis-à-vis the white business executive opens the way to the qualitatively heightened exploitation of the jazz musician, the disdain with which the former regards the latter makes such exploitation a virtual certainty. Although I will present the bulk of the evidence that substantiates this assertion in chapters 3 and 4, one particularly vivid example at this point may be useful in linking this chapter with what follows.

While living in Los Angeles in 1946, saxophonist Charlie Parker, the founding father of bebop, underwent a psychological breakdown, was arrested and then sentenced for six months to Camarillo State Hospital for the mentally ill. As the period of his court-ordered confinement wore on, Parker became increasingly restive and began threatening to attempt escape. To forestall that possibility, Ross Russell, the owner of Dial Records, a company whose raison d'être was to record Parker's music, "dug through the state mental hygiene code and found an alternative: upon recommendation of a board in Sacramento, it was possible for an [out-of-state] inmate to be released into the custody of an approved California resident. . . ."[7]

Accordingly, after arranging for the necessary bureaucratic paper-shuffling, Russell was able to have the saxophonist discharged in his custody. Before Parker was released, however, Russell made certain to obtain, as a quid pro quo, the artist's signature on a renewal of his exclusive recording contract with Dial. Not that this prevented the executive from complaining subsequently, with considerable disingenuousness, that "this matter" became "the source of later bad feeling, Charlie contending that I 'wouldn't let him out until he signed the paper.'"[8]

Parker's grasp of the situation, of course, was completely accurate. To bring into clearer focus how his powerlessness and

Russell's evident willingness to take advantage of it resulted in the victimization of the musician, it is only necessary to ask a single rhetorical question: what would have been the outcome had a record-company owner sought to impose such a contract on a white concert artist of comparable stature—a Glenn Gould, for example, or a Van Cliburn—as his price for securing the artist's discharge from a mental hospital? The ensuing hue and cry, I dare say, would have frozen any such scheme in its tracks and caused the perpetrator to be roundly denounced as a miserable wretch, heartless scoundrel, ad infinitum. But because Charlie Parker was a black jazz artist, Russell could be quite certain that no one would lift a finger in his behalf, even if all the details of this repulsive episode ultimately became public. After all, what influential newspaper would care to expend so much as a couple of inches of newsprint on the matter? What radio commentator would devote thirty seconds to a discussion of the fate of some doubtless half-crazed nigger dope addict locked up in the local mad house?

Thus was Charlie Parker's contract with Dial Records renewed. The artist understood only too well that to get himself out of Camarillo, he had no alternative but to swallow whatever terms Ross Russell chose to dictate—and he would have no recourse to higher authorities should the producer see fit to capitalize on his vulnerability. In the history of white control of black music, as the next two chapters demonstrate, this incident is atypical only in that the details have since come to light.

The double standard. In view of the foregoing, it should be no surprise to learn that white executives in the recording industry maintain a double standard where white and black art are involved. As I recount at length in chapter 4, white executives see the former as precious, sublime, and eminently worthy of support; the qualities of the latter, conversely, they see as just the opposite.

Ideological mystification. The same white executives who occupy the command posts in the political economy of jazz are also in a position to shape and direct the manufacture and dissemination of ideas about jazz: ideas about who creates the music, ideas about who benefits from its creation, ideas about which political notions on the subject are acceptable, and—patently of great importance—ideas about those issues that deserve discussion and those that merit only a prompt and permanent burial. Hence the ability to determine the production and distribution of ideas in jazz obviously reinforces the power of those who already control the production and distribution of the music itself. Because of its unmistakable significance, then, I have devoted the second section of this book to a consideration of this ideological domination of the political economy of jazz. Chapter 5, introductory in nature, surveys the pervasive intellectual dishonesty that has characterized the work of many of the best-known white writers on jazz; chapter 6 is a study in some depth of one particular work by such an author; and in chapter 7 I advance my counterproposal for an approach to the writing of jazz history that is divorced from apologetics for an inequitable status quo.

✻

In the preceding paragraphs, I have tried to summarize in schematic form the essential features of the political economy of jazz. In the pages that follow, I attempt to clothe this barebones outline with as much evidence as I have been able to amass. Admittedly, my treatment is at opposite poles from that of Nat Hentoff and the great majority of other white writers on jazz; I leave it to the reader to judge which approach comes closer to doing the subject justice.

NOTES

1. Nat Hentoff, *Jazz Is* (New York: Avon Books, 1978).
2. Frank Kofsky, *Black Nationalism and the Revolution in Music* (New York: Pathfinder Press, 1970).

3. Martin Williams, *The Jazz Tradition* (New York: Oxford University Press, 1970).

4. Quoted in *Jazz Is*, p. 257.

5. See, for example, LeRoi Jones (Amiri Baraka), *Black Music* (New York: William Morrow, 1968), p. 11, and Frank Kofsky, *John Coltrane and the Jazz Revolution of the 1960s*, the expanded and revised edition of *Black Nationalism and the Revolution in Music* (New York: Pathfinder Press, 1997), chapter 5.

6. Coleman is quoted in A.B. Spellman, *Four Lives in the Bebop Business* (New York: Random House, 1966), pp. 129–131.

7. Ross Russell, *Bird Lives!: The High Life and Hard Times of Charlie (Yardbird) Parker* (New York: Charterhouse, 1975), pp. 232–33.

8. Ibid., p. 234. Oscar Goodstein, owner of the Birdland nightclub in New York during the late 1940s and the 1950s, took similar advantage of pianist Bud Powell's mental illness.

2

Why let a little thing like death interfere with exploitation?

Some years ago, a musician friend, drummer Jimmy Robinson of Sacramento,* made mention of the problems that a colleague of his, San Francisco pianist Mark Levine, was encountering in trying to hold Catalyst Records to the terms of its contract with him. (This contract is reprinted in full in Appendix A.) Robinson had played on Levine's one Catalyst album, *Up 'Til Now* (Catalyst CAT-7614), and was anticipating working on the next as well. But although the pianist's contract called for a total of three albums to be released over a two-year period, the company was being evasive when he sought to learn its plans for additional recording sessions.

At this point, I checked with Mark Levine himself, who verified what Jimmy Robinson had told me, but asked me not to write anything about the subject for a few months, until his

---

* Jimmy Robinson not only pointed me in the direction of some of the information presented in this chapter, but also encouraged me to incorporate it into a systematic treatment of the political economy of the jazz-recording business. It is a pleasure to have this opportunity to acknowledge my indebtedness to him.

contract with Catalyst either was honored in the recording studio or breached (by being allowed to expire without additional recordings) by the company. Naturally, I complied.

Months passed. The expiration date of Levine's contract came and went without so much as a word out of Catalyst, despite the numerous letters and telephone calls with which he besieged that firm. By the time the pianist and I discussed the subject again, therefore, he was willing to speak for attribution about his experiences with various recording companies, Catalyst included. Some of what he related I will discuss in this chapter, some I will defer until the next.*

The first thing I asked Levine was what he planned to do now that Catalyst had refused to honor its contract. The answer was short and sour: nothing. His only possible recourse, he explained, was to hire an attorney and sue the company for violation of contract. But no attorney would take such a case unless the client could make a healthy payment in advance, and if Levine possessed that amount of money, he would have had no need for Catalyst in the first place—he could have recorded one or more albums himself and arranged for distribution through any of several different companies.

The worst part of his dealings with Catalyst, he continued, was not that the firm failed to record the two additional albums called for in his contract, but that "I lost two years out of my career while Catalyst kept me on the hook." If, in other words, Catalyst had been good enough to communicate its intentions, at least the pianist could have begun shopping around for a different contract; but no, the firm did not have even that elementary degree of decency. As a result, Levine was impaled "on the hook" for two years, uncertain whether Catalyst planned to live up to its contract and therefore unwilling to break the contract himself by opening negotiations with a second company.

---

* That I am grateful to Mark Levine for being so helpful in supplying me with information and corroborating documents probably goes without saying. Obviously, my treatment of the topic would have been much weaker without his aid.

In addition, Levine also was unhappy with the royalty payments he had received—or, rather, not received—from Catalyst. The company had paid him artist's royalties based on total sales of 600 albums; but upon checking with four record stores in Berkeley (Tower, Leopold's, Odyssey, and Berrigan's, the last two now defunct), he learned that 450 copies of *Up 'Til Now* had been sold *in that city alone,* not taking into account San Francisco, Oakland and the remainder of Northern California. What is more, the company had paid out neither the publishing nor the "airplay" royalties due Levine from the three of his compositions he had copublished with Catalyst, whereas the one piece that Levine had published himself already had produced publishing royalties transmitted by the Harry Fox Agency and payment for "airplay" transmitted by Broadcast Music, Incorporated (BMI).*

My next step was to hear what Catalyst had to say regarding these allegations. To that end, I made a series of telephone calls to the company's headquarters in Los Angeles, where I spoke with Mr. Pat Britt, who had produced most of the jazz albums on that label, Levine's included. Britt acknowledged that Catalyst had not fulfilled the pianist's contract and that he had not received the various kinds of royalty and other payments owed him. His ostensible explanation was that (1) the company had been sold by its original parent firm, Springboard International, to a second owner, LTD Productions; (2) the latter did not wish to honor contracts signed under the regime of the former; and (3) the former was unwilling to release funds now legally the property of the latter.

Given that firms constantly are bought and sold without their previous obligations being repudiated, I must say that I do not find this "explanation" of why Catalyst violated its contract with Mark Levine notably persuasive. But even if one is willing to

---

* The Harry Fox Agency, as I explain more fully in the following chapter, collects royalties due songwriters from recording companies; BMI does the same with respect to royalties for "airplay" from radio and television stations.

swallow such a flimsy excuse, several questions still remain un-answered. After LTD Productions decided not to be bound by contracts signed by representatives of Catalyst when it was still owned by Springboard International, for instance, why did the company fail to notify all the artists then affiliated with the label? That, at any rate, would have allowed them to search for new contracts. Or again, why did Catalyst not inform artists and songwriters that royalties owed them were tied up in a dispute between the old and the new owners of the recording company?

One could easily extend the list of such questions—but to what purpose? No matter what inquires we care to make, the answer will be the same: all but the most renowned jazz artists are virtually defenseless against a recording company—and, by extension, a concert or festival promoter, a nightclub owner, a booking agency—that chooses to do them dirt. Only those per-formers whose financial positions are so secure and/or whose services are so in demand that companies are reluctant to risk incurring their wrath are immune to the operation of this rule. You are not likely to need your fingers and toes to compute the number who answer to this description.

In one sense, though, I suppose it would be possible to argue that the all-too-typical details of Mark Levine's cavalier treat-ment by Catalyst Records shows that "progress" of a sort has taken place. Fifty or sixty years ago, when the recording busi-ness was just emerging from its infancy, such high-handed and unjust dealings were for the most part reserved for black per-formers. In our much-more-enlightened times, however, we have advanced to the point where jazz musicians of all colors are victimized with fine impartiality by the recording industry. Indeed, the situation in that industry is reminiscent in more than one sense of the last line of Lenny Bruce's satiric monologue on sharks: "They're thoroughly integrated. Everyone goes—mop, mop and that's *it!*"

But although it may be the case that jazz-oriented businesses are now, like the sharks, "thoroughly integrated," it is nonethe-less true that in order to understand contemporary practices, we must view them in historical perspective, keeping in mind the full measure of contempt with which white-owned companies traditionally have approached "their" black labor force (a topic I explore at greater length in chapter 3). Only in this way will we be able to grasp how and why a jazz recording firm, for example, can still proceed in this day and age to plunder musicians in the most blithe, carefree, and casual fashion, like Elizabethan freebooters falling upon a treasure ship bursting with bullion.

There is no better way of illustrating this history of continuous victimization of the artist than by a consideration of the late John Hammond's strenuous feats in the field of black music on behalf of himself and his longtime employer, Columbia Records. In most jazz circles, Hammond's name is uttered in tones of utmost reverence—not surprising, when one notes how assiduously its possessor labored to assure himself of canonization as St. John the Second while still alive. Some excerpts from his correspondence with me will convey the tirelessness with which he sought to inflate his reputation as, among other things, the protector of black people in general and black artists in particular: "I have been through a lot in trying to make for breakthroughs for Negro musicians."[1] "I feel so strongly about gradualism that after thirty years [!] on the Board and as Vice President of the NAACP, I resigned last Fall because of the fact that I feel Roy Wilkins['s] tie-up with the [Lyndon B. Johnson] administration is not the way to achieve progress and justice for minorities."[2] And so on, ad infinitum.

The overwhelming majority of those authors who write about jazz have shown little inclination to dispute the grandeur of Hammond's achievements—as recounted, of course, by the master himself. And small wonder. As a descendant of the Vanderbilt family on the one hand and as an upper-echelon executive with Columbia Records for decades prior to his retirement on the other, Hammond was a man in whose person great wealth and power were combined. Few were so foolhardy as to risk incurring his displeasure; those who did quickly learned that one does not flout the wishes of The Great Man with impunity.

Take, as a representative instance, the case of Billie Holiday. Relations between blacks and whites during the 1930s, by and large, were still marked by deference on the part of the former toward the latter, especially when the white person in question was as unmistakably affluent and influential as Hammond. Regardless of what they may have thought about him in private, therefore, almost all black (and many white) musicians of that period were reluctant to defy his wishes openly. Billie Holiday, however, was an exception. Ass-kissing, if I may put it bluntly, was never her strong suit—and it made little difference whether the ass in question belonged to John Hammond or John Doe.

Given Hammond's expectations of deference as his due, a falling-out between the two was near-inevitable. The inevitable in fact occurred in 1938. Without providing all the pertinent details, Hammond recounts in his autobiography how he turned on Billie Holiday when she committed the sin of displeasing him. Holiday, it seems,

> had hired as her manager a woman from a distinguished family I knew well. I was concerned that she and her family might be hurt by unsavory gossip, or even blackmailed by the gangsters and dope pushers Billie knew.
>
> It was one of the few times in my life when I felt compelled to interfere in a personal relationship which was none of my business. I told the manager's family what I knew and what I feared. Soon afterward the manager and Billie broke up, and Billie never worked at Cafe Society again. I think she never forgave me for what she suspected was my part in the breakup. . . .[3]

When the emperor can marshal power of that magnitude and does not scruple to use it to jeopardize a performer's livelihood, few indeed will be eager to proclaim the true nature of his new clothes. And fewer still among black artists, whose fortunes in the best of cases are already sufficiently precarious. That fact goes a great distance toward explaining why there has been so little public discussion by musicians of the less savory aspects of the career of St. John the Second.

Nevertheless, here and there some of the dirty linen has found its way into daylight. None of it is more edifying, if we wish to understand the political economy of white domination of black music, than the tangled relationship of John Hammond and Columbia Records to Bessie Smith.

The first and most important point to emphasize is that, as author Chris Albertson reveals in his biography of Bessie Smith, Hammond signed the singer to a series of contracts with Columbia Records that gave her a small fixed fee for each performance she recorded *and no royalties*.[4] Such contracts were apparently standard practice with the executive, for Billie Holiday unequivocally stated in her autobiography, *Lady Sings the Blues*: "Later on John Hammond paired me up with Teddy Wilson and his band for another record session. This time I got thirty bucks for making half a dozen sides."[5] What is more, when she protested about this arrangement, it was, according to her, a Columbia executive named Bernie Hanighen—and not John Hammond—"who really went to bat for me" and "almost lost his job at Columbia fighting for me."*[6] Subsequently, Holiday reiterated that although she "made over two hundred sides between 1933 and 1944" for John Hammond at Columbia, she didn't "get a cent of royalties on any of them." "The only royalties I get," she explained, "are on my records made after I signed with Decca."[7]

In itself, the fact that Hammond was, to put it mildly, a willing accomplice in signing both Bessie Smith and Billie Holiday to no-royalty agreements is bad enough.[8] What makes it one hundred times worse is that "company policy" at Columbia Records now designates Hammond "the sole recipient of royalties from sales of Bessie Smith's recent [early 1970s] reissue albums."[9] So, incredible as it may seem, during his later years

---

* It may have been to revenge himself for Holiday's complaints about the contract with Columbia he imposed on her that Hammond discouraged the "woman from a distinguished family" from becoming the singer's manager.

this descendant of the Vanderbilt line was further enriched by a black woman who came into this world in near-penniless circumstances and who lay, as we shall see, in an unmarked grave for more than thirty years. There, in a nutshell, one has the political economy of jazz stripped to its essence.

In 1973 I attempted to estimate how much money Hammond had by then gained from the sales of recordings by Bessie Smith, using as the basis of this calculation figures supplied by Hammond himself in an interview published in the March 4, 1971, issue of *down beat*. Thanks to what Albertson calls "unprecedented advance publicity for reissues,"[10] Hammond was able to boast that the "success" of the reissue discs was likewise "absolutely unprecedented." What this translated to in 1973 dollars was, at a conservative figure, about $60,000 for Hammond himself—and in 1990s dollars, an amount *at least* four or five times as great. Could it have been to insure this result, do you suppose, that Columbia Records "prepared for it [the release of the Bessie Smith albums] by a lot of advance publicity," something that, to continue quoting Hammond's own words on the subject of reissue recordings, "we ordinarily never do."[11]

(Again striving to guarantee that he would be seen only in the most favorable light, Hammond later muddied the waters by denying that he was ever "paid any *incentive* bonus for the many reissues of Columbia records I produced back in the 1930s [my emphasis]."[12] With respect to Albertson's research on the subject of *artist's royalties*, though, he maintained a discreet silence. In his shoes, wouldn't you?)

Yet not even this concludes the matter. There is, I regret to say, more—much more—to this illuminating, if sordid, tale. At the same time that he was binding Bessie Smith and Billie Holiday to agreements that earned no royalties on record sales for either performer, Hammond added insult to injury by mounting a Herculean effort to have the American Federation of Musicians nullify the contract that Count Basie had signed with a competitor, Decca Records. The grounds on which he sought to have Basie's contract with Decca overturned was that it was, as he put it, "typical of some of the underscale deals which record companies imposed on unsophisticated Negro and 'country' artists"![13] There may be instances of greater gall or balder effrontery, but if so, I hope never to encounter them. Talk about "underscale deals . . . imposed on unsophisticated Negro . . . artists"! If that isn't the very description of Hammond's own dealings with Bessie Smith and Billie Holiday, I would like to know what is.

If the foregoing suggests that those who sit astride the political economy of jazz do not put too high a premium on either truthfulness or equity, the sequel only underlines that conclusion more forcefully. One might think that death, at least, would suffice to rescue even black artists from further exploitation. In the case of John Hammond, Columbia Records and Bessie Smith, however, such a surmise proves to be too optimistic by half.

One of those things that "everyone knows" is that Bessie Smith died following an automobile accident in the deep South because, in that day of rampant segregation, she could not obtain medical treatment at a nearby hospital reserved for white patients. But as not infrequently happens, what "everyone knows" in this case turns out to be quite wrong, as Albertson demonstrates in chapter 11 of *Bessie*. Where, then, did this story originate?

With none other than John Hammond, it now appears. As Albertson observes, "The widespread controversy over the circumstances surrounding Bessie's death did not arise until the following month [after the event], when *down beat* magazine printed an article by John Hammond."[14] In that article, after reciting the now-familiar version of how the singer met her demise, but (not surprisingly) providing no evidence to support his allegations, Hammond came to the point in his final paragraph:

> Be that as it may, the UHCA [United Hot Clubs of America, a Columbia subsidiary] is busy sponsoring a special Bessie Smith memorial album . . . [that] will be released by Brunswick-

Columbia around the middle of November with pictures of the performers and details about each of the discs. Take it from one who cherished all the records that this will be the best buy of the year in music.[15]

Never one to let mere questions of taste or respect for the dead interfere with a chance to promote his fame and fortune, evidently Hammond himself either invented or else disseminated without verifying a wholly fictitious account of the death of Bessie Smith, the sole purpose of which was to obtain some free—and very sensational—advertising for the impending release of recordings that he had produced. As Hammond admitted to Chris Albertson "with some embarrassment," his article in *down beat* "was based entirely on hearsay," and "a few phone calls, made at the time," could readily have determined what actually had transpired and "might have curbed the circulating rumors."[16] But ascertaining truth and curbing rumors were, on the face of it, absolutely the least of Hammond's concerns. Whether most of us will experience life after death remains a moot point. But for such black artists as Bessie Smith, the persistence of victimization by a white-owned recording company after death is a virtual certainty.*

---

* Even if, as in the case of John Coltrane, the artist has not recorded for John Hammond. In July 1967 I was in New York to attend funeral services for Coltrane, and while there I met Hammond for the first time. Over lunch, he informed me of his plans to release as a "John Coltrane Memorial album" a forthcoming recording by saxophonist John Handy that, utterly by coincidence, contained Handy's reading of Coltrane's composition "Naima." After some reflection, I decided I had no choice but to write an editorial statement for the September 1967 issue of *Jazz* that, without mentioning any names, outlined Hammond's scheme and then denounced "this sort of disgusting eagerness to capitalize on what must be the greatest setback imaginable" to jazz. Evidently, this shaft found its intended target, for the John Handy album in question was released with the title *New View!* (Columbia 9497), and the sole reference to Coltrane was confined to the phrase "In Memory of John Coltrane" that appeared in small type and parentheses following the listing of "Naima" in the program printed on the album jacket. As one might expect, however, my relationship with John Hammond did not survive this incident.

As a by-product of the massive wave of publicity unleashed by Columbia Records to promote the sales of the Bessie Smith recordings it reissued at the start of the 1970s, it was discovered that Bessie Smith herself was buried in an unmarked grave. The ensuing hue and cry ultimately led two people, the late rock singer Janis Joplin and Juanita Green, a black nurse from Philadelphia who as a child had scrubbed floors for Bessie Smith, to raise a few hundred dollars for a headstone and a scholarship in the black artist's name. One year later, Columbia Records finally saw fit to part with one thousand dollars to augment this fund. To this sum John Hammond then magnanimously added his own princely contribution—fifty dollars.

Both during her lifetime and after it, John Hammond enriched himself and enhanced his reputation greatly as a result of his association with Bessie Smith. In financial terms alone he derived, at a conservative estimate, more than $200,000 (in current dollars) from his involvement with her. That he was willing to return only a paltry $50—0.025 percent of $200,000—to commemorate her burial site illustrates more eloquently than any amount of words the concept of just compensation for black artists that prevails among those white executives in whose grasp lies everything worth controlling in the political economy of jazz.

NOTES

1. John Hammond to the author, May 29, 1967.
2. John Hammond to the author, June 2, 1967.
3. John Hammond and Irving Townshend, *John Hammond on Record* (New York: Ridge Press/Summit Books, 1977), pp. 208–09.
4. Chris Albertson, *Bessie* (New York: Stein & Day, 1972), pp. 184–85, 227–29.
5. Billie Holiday and William Dufty, *Lady Sings the Blues* (New York: Lancer Books, 1965), p. 38.
6. *Ibid.*
7. *Ibid.*, p. 166.

8. Characteristically concerned to prevent his reputation from being tarnished, Hammond claimed that all along he was attempting to secure a better contract for Bessie Smith (*John Hammond on Record*, p. 122). Fortunately for him, none of the principals were alive to dispute this assertion; significantly, however, it receives no confirmation in Albertson's biography of the singer, and that author also flatly contradicts Hammond's account in several places, for instance: "No one who knew Bessie in 1933 believes Hammond's story of meeting Bessie in a speakeasy . . ." (*Bessie*, p. 184).

9. Albertson, *Bessie*, p. 185, n. 5.

10. Albertson, *Bessie*, p. 232.

11. Both quotations of Hammond come from an interview with him in *down beat*, March 4, 1971; details of the calculation of his gains from royalties on the Bessie Smith recordings are in my 1973 Ph.D. dissertation in history at the University of Pittsburgh, "Black Nationalism and the Revolution in Music: Social Change and Stylistic Development in the Music of John Coltrane and Others, 1954–1967," pp. 371–74.

12. *John Hammond on Record*, p. 377.

13. Hammond is quoted on pp. 139–40 of Ross Russell, *Jazz Style in Kansas City and the Southwest* (Berkeley and Los Angeles: University of California Press, 1971).

14. Albertson, *Bessie*, p. 216.

15. Quoted in *ibid.*, p. 216.

16. Albertson, *Bessie*, p. 217.

3

'Selling records to colored people': white contempt for black art

In the preceding chapter I presented a very small fraction of the evidence demonstrating a pattern of exploitation of black musical artists—and, by extension, of white artists who perform in black idioms—that extends at least from the 1920s to the present day. Looking over this dismal historical record, it may seem plausible to assert that corporate behavior of this sort arises out of nothing more than naked greed: business executives wish to increase their profits, jazz artists are vulnerable, Q.E.D.

In actuality, however, while such an ostensible explanation makes good economic determinism, it is poor historical reasoning. Merely because one group is more powerful than another, it does not follow that members of the first invariably take advantage of this situation to victimize those of the second. Parents ordinarily nurture children. The sighted usually do not steal from the blind. Older siblings routinely care for and protect younger ones. Granted that none of the foregoing generalizations is ironclad and exceptions do occur, it nonetheless remains true that a disparity in power between two groups need not inevitably lead to the oppression of the weaker by the stronger.

What clearly is the case, though, is that when an imbalance of power between two groups is combined with a situation in which the more powerful views the less powerful with contempt, the latter unfortunates are likely to suffer—grievously. Anyone who has read more than casually about the traditional attitude of the English and Anglo-American elite with respect to the poor, the laboring classes, the Irish, and peoples of color will experience no difficulty in calling to mind a wealth of doleful facts that illustrate this lamentable reality.[1]

The relevance of this point for an analysis of the political economy of jazz is simply this: white executives in the recording industry, as I will bring out in some detail momentarily, tend to regard those artists who perform in black musical idioms with scorn. It is this scorn that "legitimates"—in the eyes of the executives, at any rate—the type of shoddy treatment of black artists that was the subject of the previous chapter.

But more than that, this same contempt, as I will demonstrate in chapter 4, promotes the creation of a double standard, according to which art music in the European tradition is considered important, prestigious, and worthy of economic support—"classical," in a word—while art music in the Afro-American tradition is denigrated as trivial, base, aesthetically worthless, and tolerable only insofar as profitable. Thus, as one consequence, white artists who perform the symphonic repertoire will not be victimized, regardless of their vulnerability, to anything like the same degree as are jazz artists—indicating once more, incidentally, that economic determinism does not offer an adequate basis on which to interpret the world. And, as another consequence, not only will jazz artists be shortchanged in comparison with European concert artists, but the very *music* of the former will be disparaged and even damaged by the white executives who hold it in such low esteem.

Reserving a full-scale discussion of this last assertion for the next chapter, at this point I want to return to the subject of that contempt-from-above that, in my estimation, permeates relations between white recording-company executives and jazz musicians. I will take as my point of departure the general observation that if artists have encountered profound difficulties in obtaining respect in a business-ruled culture whose yardstick is the dollar, and if black people have had their claim to a common humanity rejected in a hierarchical, white-Protestant-dominated society, it only stands to reason that the serious black artist in any medium can expect to reap a double harvest of disdain as the fruit of his or her labor. (If, moreover, the medium happens to be one *created* by blacks, the degree of disdain may be even greater yet.)

And it is just such disdain (sometimes mingled with fear) that from the beginning has characterized the recording industry's approach to black music. To document this assertion, we need look no further than those small firms that have specialized in the production of jazz, blues, gospel, and other "race" recordings by black artists. Although some of these companies, to be sure, may have been started and operated by individuals with a sincere and abiding interest in black music, most have either commenced or else quickly degenerated into vehicles for the taking of profits at the expense of the artist.

The example of Prestige Records, established by Bob Weinstock in 1949 and sold by him to Fantasy Records in 1971, well illustrates the rule. So odious was the reputation of this firm by the middle of the 1950s, a mere half-dozen or so years after its birth, that Miles Davis, for one, advised younger musicians just arriving in New York to contract with any other company save that one. It was notorious in jazz circles that Weinstock habitually took advantage of musicians who were desperate for money—often because of an addiction to heroin—by signing them to contracts requiring them to record a huge number of selections in exchange for a minute advance against future royalty payments, with the latter set at an unconscionably low rate to boot. In this fashion, his company was able to accumulate innumerable priceless performances by Davis, Sonny Rollins, Thelonious Monk, John Coltrane, Charlie Parker, Eric Dolphy, and too many others even to attempt naming.

A very young Jackie McLean also affiliated himself with Prestige early in the 1950s, and, according to A.B. Spellman, the saxophonist later concluded that this was "one of the greatest mistakes he has ever made." "If you can imagine being under the Nazi regime and not knowing it," McLean explained,

> then you've got an idea of what it's like to be with that company. I was starving when I signed that contract. The baby was being born, so I was glad to get my name on a record and make some money. And my condition [as a heroin addict] didn't help either. . . . Everybody made that move—Miles [Davis] was with that company, Sonny Rollins, John Coltrane, and [Thelonious] Monk. They all got out of it as soon as they could, just as I did.
>
> It's a perfect example of giving everything and getting nothing back. They give you a little bit of front money [advance against future royalties], and then they tell you about the royalties you are going to get after the record is released. I did a million dates for them, and all it amounted to is that I paid for the whole thing: engineers, the notes on the back of the album, the color photograph, the whole thing, out of my money. I still get statements saying that I owe that company ridiculous sums like $50,000; I'm exaggerating, but it's not much less ridiculous than that.

McLean is convinced that companies such as Prestige are fully "aware of what the cat's problems are. If they weren't aware that there aren't many jazz clubs going and that record dates are a necessity to many musicians and that some musicians use drugs," he reasons,

> there would be more jazz musicians around with money. Certainly the record companies are making money on the jazz that they produce. They're not signing anybody with any company that's not making money. They're not making records for the sake of Allah, they're making records to make money. But all

they ever do when you go to them and ask them for some money you figure you've got coming to you, they just tell you that things are bad, that this or that album didn't do too good.[2]

In light of these scathing revelations by Jackie McLean, it comes as no surprise to learn that, far from being even slightly grateful to the black artists who made Prestige so prosperous, Bob Weinstock despised them—indeed, almost openly so. Bob Porter, who went to work for the company in the middle of the 1960s, has written that by the end of the decade, Weinstock was spending "less and less time at the office" and "had musicians on the label whom he had never met."[3] During the several years that Porter was in his employ, Weinstock

came to the studio only once, to welcome back Gene Ammons [from prison]. By now he didn't like to meet musicians, feeling they'd just bug him for money. It had become impossible for him to be a [jazz] fan. . . . [B]y 1970, the delicate balance between fan and businessman had tipped completely.
In the direction of the latter, clearly.

Given this sequence of events, the denouement was wholly predictable: "Weinstock," Porter notes, "is completely out of music now and into Florida real estate."[4] In his present exalted position, one can be certain that the former owner of Prestige Recordings does not waste much of his time thinking of those black musicians who so obligingly made possible his second career, still less pondering the vast disparity between the fate of many of them—early death, frequently in the most abject circumstances—and his own.

For overall insensitivity and scornfulness towards black artists, however, the achievements of Herman Lubinsky, who founded Savoy Records in 1947, appear to eclipse even those of Bob Weinstock. Again, we are indebted for our information to Bob Porter, who compiled and annotated *The Roots of Rock 'N' Roll* (Savoy SJL 2221) from the archives of Lubinsky's firm.

Where Bob Weinstock had been "a fan" at the outset, Lubinsky never displayed even that much respect for black music of any type. "He was in his mid-forties when he started Savoy Records as an adjunct to his thriving electronic parts business," Porter relates. Lubinsky's firm was located "in a Black area of Newark, New Jersey," and although he began by recording a variety of musics, it was "jazz, blues, gospel" on which he soon

> decided to concentrate. . . . As he mentioned frequently in his correspondence, he was trying to "sell records to colored people." Rumor has it that Lubinsky once got rid of a promising group when he discovered [!] that the group was White.[5]

Savoy's owner made no pretense whatsoever of regarding black music as art; to him it was merely a commodity, something that could be sold for a profit just like any other item in his stock. "He was not a music man," Porter relates,

> and rarely went into the studio. He was a businessman and (where black music was concerned) very tight with a buck. By all accounts, he was one tough SOB to deal with.

One can be sure of it.

Lubinsky's contempt for black music, its artists, and its audience, emerged, like that of Bob Weinstock, in a multitude of ways. Most revealing of all, though, was his unwillingness to develop any understanding—appreciation, of course, was entirely out of the question—of the art that brought him such lucrative returns. Bob Porter narrates the following instructive incident:

> "The Hucklebuck" was one of the biggest instrumentals of the 1940s, and was covered [recorded] by dozens of different artists. Oddly, the record was almost rejected! When Lubinsky heard a trumpet [solo] . . . instead of saxophone, he was furious. Fortunately [for him], cooler heads prevailed.

And Herman Lubinsky was thus rescued from the consequences of his own willful ignorance and folly. It was neither the first time nor the last.

The entrepreneur was similarly deaf to the merits of "Double Crossing Blues," a 78-rpm disc by the Johnny Otis group, Little Esther Phillips and the Robbins: "This was another [hit] record Lubinsky didn't like [and] was planning to reject," Porter explains,

> when Bill Cook of a Newark radio station, WAAT, heard it and flipped out. When Cook first put it on the air, the song didn't even have a title. But the phone calls to the station were so heavy that a contest was held to name the performance and "Double Crossing Blues" won.

What more can one say of a businessman whose success at recording and selling black music was as great as his comprehension of it was abysmal? Only this: that the scarcely disguised disdain for black art that Lubinsky consistently manifested is all too typical of what exists among white executives in the recording industry.

Further evidence of the pervasive nature of this disdain comes from my own experiences in that industry. During the years of 1967 to 1969—when the several federal agencies charged with protecting the citizenry from perils within and without were doing their utmost to prevent the security of this republic from being endangered by my being allowed to teach at an institution of higher learning—I managed to survive by a variety of stratagems.[6] One of these was intermittent work in minor capacities for Bob Thiele, who became my occasional employer while still the director of Artists and Repertoire at Impulse Records, a subsidiary of ABC Records. Subsequently, Thiele left ABC to establish his own Flying Dutchman label, and I went on his payroll for a short time, until a series of unbridgeable differences on a multitude of issues brought us to a final split.

Within the jazz world, Bob Thiele is known primarily through his association with John Coltrane during the last six years of the saxophonist's life (1961–1967), when he was under contract to Impulse Records. And certainly Thiele did everything within his power to capitalize on that association, even to the point of having photographs that showed the two men appearing to confer printed prominently on the covers of Coltrane's recordings. (From working for him as a photographer myself, I can attest that Thiele personally supervised every aspect of an album's production, including selection of the photographs and other artwork that ultimately graced the jacket.) For he was well aware that, as he told me in a 1968 interview,

> if I had never met Coltrane, I would be in serious trouble with respect to the real crappy economic aspects of my own career. . . . I think that I owe a lot to Coltrane.[7]

At Coltrane's urging, Thiele began recording many of the artists involved in the jazz revolution of the 1960s. In this way, he enhanced his reputation as, first, the producer of John Coltrane's albums and, second, as a recording company executive who was deeply involved with many of the artists who promised to become that decade's leading innovators. All of which, of course, was of considerable use to Thiele in dealing with "the real crappy economic aspects" of his career.

But as is so often true, there was a sizable gap between appearances and reality. In appearance, for instance, Coltrane and Thiele had an intimate and mutually supportive working relationship. In reality, Thiele "didn't know too much about him" at the time he showed up for his first recording session with Coltrane. "I had read about him and heard about him," the producer told me,

> but I hadn't really listened to him. It was sort of a rough assignment for me, in a way. . . . It was . . . tough for me because I really wasn't that familiar with his music.
>
> It was sort of a distant relationship, really. I was a, well, a little surprised at my own ability to communicate with him.[8]

As if the supposedly ferocious black saxophonist were in the habit of chewing up and swallowing a couple of white business-men for breakfast each morning!

Similarly, the image Thiele has cultivated is that of a committed champion of the jazz revolution. In fact, however, it was only because of Coltrane's unceasing efforts that the producer

> became aware of Archie Shepp and many of the younger players. When John heard any good player, he would call me and ask that I please give him some consideration. I think that if we had signed everyone that John recommended, we'd have four hundred musicians on the label.[9]

Just because of his great dependence on Coltrane, however, as soon as the saxophonist was no longer alive to shape Thiele's taste, the executive began to flounder in a sea of musical vapidity, focusing his efforts on recording a group of Southern California rock-oriented white musicians (such as saxophonist Tom Scott) who made their livelihoods primarily by performing trite arrangements in Hollywood recording studios, as opposed to creating jazz improvisations before flesh-and-blood audiences. At the same time, Thiele was constantly being importuned (by myself, among others) to offer contracts to such innovative figures as pianists McCoy Tyner and Cecil Taylor, saxophonists Ornette Coleman, Sam Rivers and John Gilmore, trumpeter-composer Bill Dixon, and many other performers who were not affiliated with any firm and whose music was consequently going unrecorded. To these urgings, Thiele had a stock reply (which he used often enough for me to commit to memory): "I can't work with those guys like Archie and Ornette any more," he would complain, "they're getting too militant."*

* I quoted this statement in an article, "Black Roots Grow in L.A. [Los Angeles] Ghetto," *Changes,* September 1, 1971, p. 11, and sent a copy to Bob Thiele to make sure that he had an opportunity to reply. No such reply was ever forthcoming.

I confess I was incredulous the first time I heard these words. Could this be *Bob Thiele* speaking, the same Bob Thiele who had produced so many albums by avant-garde artists like John Coltrane, Archie Shepp, Albert Ayler, Marion Brown? Evidently, it could. More than that—it was.

In retrospect, it seems that Thiele had been able to collaborate harmoniously with the Shepps and Aylers only so long as Coltrane was available to serve as an intermediary or buffer. Hence once Coltrane had died, Thiele's relations with the younger black jazz performers began to degenerate, as witness his assertion that he could not "work with those guys any more" because they had become "too militant." My impression is that, notwithstanding his affable demeanor, Bob Thiele expected, perhaps without even being cognizant of it, some degree of deference from those artists he chose to record. This expectation may not have posed a problem in his dealings with musicians of earlier generations, but the rebellious performers of the 1960s were definitely a different breed—and deference was hardly their forte. What Thiele may have regarded as a question of deference and, ultimately, control the musicians more than likely viewed as a question of black pride and artistic integrity—issues on which they were not about to compromise. The stage was thus set for a confrontation; its near-certain outcome was a parting of the ways as soon as this latent conflict became manifest. As soon, in other words, as John Coltrane was no longer present to smooth relations between corporate managers and "militants."*

---

* Is it only coincidental, one must ask, that Bob Thiele's lament about the younger black performers is echoed by an even better-known producer of jazz recordings? John Hammond expressed his distaste for avant-garde jazz performers in the following terms:

"What they're putting down really doesn't make that much sense to me. When you throw out tonality and certain disciplines, you're left with not enough. *A record supervisor is not really in control of a session like that. . . . You just have to give them their heads*" [*down beat*, March 4, 1971, p. 13; my italics]. For white executives accustomed to deference from, and control over, "their" black artists,

Another chance remark made the nature of Thiele's ambivalence about black musicians still more clear. In attending several of the recording sessions he supervised in Hollywood, I
couldn't help being struck by how few black studio musicians
he employed (one or two out of fifteen or twenty, on the average). As soon as an opportunity presented itself, therefore, I
asked him why. After a few disingenuous efforts at shifting the
responsibility to the contractors,[10] Thiele finally blurted out that
he would be "horrified"—the word was expelled with such ve-
hemence that I would have difficulty ever forgetting it—to walk
into a studio at the start of a session and see nothing but black
musicians, because, he maintained, "they can't read well enough."[*]

What made this remark so completely ludicrous is that Thiele
had been in the business of producing records for nearly three
decades at the moment he uttered it, and presumably in all that
time his powers of observation should have sufficed to give the
lie to such crude stereotypes. Except that any ideology embraced
with sufficient fervor has the power to overcome whole mountains of contrary evidence. There are, after all, people who will
be happy to inform you that the earth is flat, a man has never
walked on the moon, the Holocaust did not take place, and
heaven only knows what else.

In similar fashion, Bob Thiele was able to maintain his scorn-
ful attitude toward black musicianship on the one hand while
making use of that same musicianship to turn a profit on the
other. Presumably in order to give an album called *The Soul of
Bonnie and Clyde* (ABC Bluesway 6018) the requisite aura of
authenticity, Thiele felt compelled to employ just such an all-
black group of studio musicians as earlier he said would "hor-
rify" him. To my lot then fell a request from Thiele to write the

the notion of musicians who are so "militant" that "you just have to give them
their heads" must indeed be anathema. What we here encounter, then, is not an
idiosyncrasy but the long-established ideology of an entire social *stratum*.

[*] I quoted these words as well in my article "Black Roots," cited in full in an
earlier footnote.

notes for the album. Under ordinary circumstances, in view of the dubious concept behind the recording, I most likely would have declined the honor—but these were not ordinary circumstances. Here, as I saw it, I had a chance to drive home an important point. And indeed, even though Thiele edited my comments heavily, I was nonetheless able to emphasize the fact that the record "was cut in a pair of three-hour sessions on a single day" by black musicians, and that the arrangements had been executed "with such speed and skill that the second session finished an hour early." Then, just to remind my employer of our earlier discussion, I added, "So much for *that* particular canard."[11]

I am sure that the message reached the intended recipient—and that it made nary a dent in his thinking. For racist ideas, including the unconscious contempt that is such an integral part of them, are so deeply embedded in the mentality of most white executives in the recording industry that they can no more be expunged than a human being can survive without breathing air. Both Bob Weinstock of Prestige and Herman Lubinsky of Savoy are of Jewish descent and have, in all likelihood, middle- or working-class backgrounds. Bob Thiele, in contrast, comes from a wealthy family of German Protestants. Despite differences in origins, however, Weinstock, Lubinsky, and Thiele have in common the disdain with which they view black artists and black arts—an attitude that cuts across ethnic and class lines among white executives and thereby helps to perpetuate an ideology that unites them in their dealings with black musicians.

And that, ultimately, is why Weinstock came to prefer the respectability (such as it is) of speculating in Florida real estate to the disrepute of recording black artists. That is why Herman Lubinsky could never be bothered learning even the first thing about the music that made his fortune. That is why Bob Thiele exclaimed—only shortly before he would direct an all-black group of musicians and experience not a single difficulty—that he would be "horrified" to enter a studio full of black musicians, who "can't read well enough." If these be the patrons of black music, one shudders to think of its enemies.

In chapter 4, I will examine more thoroughly the consequences of the contempt for black artists that occurs so ubiquitously among the white businessmen who dominate the political economy of jazz. Here, meanwhile, I will close with a single illustration of what befalls the practicing jazz musician once that contempt takes concrete form.

Once more I am grateful to pianist Mark Levine, whose trials and tribulations at the hands of Catalyst Records I narrated in the previous chapter, for my information. The saga begins with Levine's involvement with an album, *Saudade*, recorded under the leadership of the Brazilian musician, Moacir Santos, for Blue Note Records. In addition to performing on *Saudade*, Levine also contributed a composition, "City of La" (often misspelled "City of LA"), which he published through his own company, Ethiopia Music. Like many other jazz musicians who are also composers, Levine retains the Harry Fox agency to collect his royalties on songs he has both written and published. As late as June 1978, the Fox Agency was told by United Artists (UA), the parent company of Blue Note Records, that a total of 2,200 copies of *Saudade* had been sold worldwide since the album's release four years prior. From his own experiences, however, the pianist had reason to believe the true figure was actually much higher. Conversations throughout the United States with other musicians who know of his work from *Saudade*, for one thing, led him to suspect that UA was deliberately under-reporting sales so as to avoid paying royalties to artists and composers. When a friend employed at UA then told Levine of an internal memorandum he had seen indicating that *Saudade* had already sold more than 40,000 copies by the fall of 1974—even as the company was claiming sales of one-twentieth of that amount in a period four times as long—those suspicions were only confirmed.

Nonetheless, Levine himself did nothing. Eventually, however, the Fox Agency was deluged with so many complaints regarding UA's nonpayment of royalties to songwriter-publishers that in 1978 it was able to compel this company to submit to an investigation of its books. The initial findings of that investigation are nothing if not instructive.

As the documents in Appendix B indicate, prior to the intervention of the Fox Agency in 1978, Mark Levine had received a total of $35.22 in royalty payments from UA and its Canadian affiliate, UA Records Ltd., for the one-year period from July 1, 1974, to June 30, 1975. But in reality, UA had misrepresented its sales figures in such a way that he was paid less than one-third of the amount legally owed him. So much emerged from the 1978 probe of UA by the Fox Agency, which in June 1978 sent him a check and an accompanying letter and sales statement (both the latter two documents are reproduced in Appendix B). The check for additional royalties was for $73.50—*more than twice the total amount UA claimed Levine's publishing company had earned.* This payment, the cover letter from the Fox Agency explained, was due the composer

> as the result of our examination of the books of United Artists Records for the period from January 1, 1973[,] to June 30, 1975.
> This portion of the recovery consists of previously unpaid royalties due on the distribution of so-called "free" records in sales plans by United Artists Records.

United Artists, in other words, had been keeping two sets of books. In the spurious set, on the basis of which the company computed artists' and composers' royalties, sales figures were systematically lowered by falsely listing as "free" records—that is, albums supplied without charge to radio stations, magazines, reviewers, and so forth—a portion of the records the company in fact sold for a profit. As companies are not required to pay any kind of royalties on such "free" records, the advantage of this mislabeling to UA is obvious.[12]

To the artist and composer who must deal with such a firm, conversely, the advantages do not appear to be correspondingly great. The sums involved overall, moreover, are anything but trifling, given the marginal existence all too many jazz musicians must endure. Let us suppose, conservatively, that Blue Note Records released an average of twenty records annually—fewer than two per month—in every year from 1966, when it was sold to United Artists by its original owners, to 1978. Suppose further that each record contained five compositions written and published by a jazz musician. Over the thirteen–year period from 1966 to 1978, there will have been a total of 1,300 such compositions recorded and published. If every Blue Note album sells one-half as well during its first year as Moacir Santos's *Saudade*, and if UA withholds royalties in the same ratio as it did with Mark Levine (paying out less than one dollar of every three owed), then the amount (in late-1970s dollars) by which musician-composers have been shortchanged comes to a total of approximately

($36.75/composition) x (5 compositions/album) x
(20 albums/year) x (13 years) = $47,775.

And this figure still probably drastically understates the situation. For one thing, I have deliberately biased on the low side my estimates both of the number of albums released per year and of sales during each album's first year. For a second, I have made no effort to take into account an album's sales during its second and subsequent years, and with some artists whose records have been issued on the Blue Note label since 1966— including McCoy Tyner, Freddie Hubbard, Elvin Jones, Herbie Hancock, Horace Silver, Art Blakey—these sales are considerable. For a third, my calculation also ignores albums originally issued before 1966 that have continued to sell well thereafter, and of these there must be dozens (for example, discs by John Coltrane, Miles Davis, Thelonious Monk, Sonny Rollins, Wayne Shorter, in addition to the musicians mentioned previously). Last, for want of reliable information I have also completely excluded any consideration of *artist's* royalties, as opposed to royalties from songwriting and publishing. But if somehow we could obtain the figures that would allow us to carry out the necessary computations, it would not surprise me if it turned out that the community of jazz musicians has been illegally deprived of at least one-half million late-1970s dollars, an amount equivalent to about two million late-1990s dollars, by one single company in one thirteen-year period. As for what the total might be if we could extend the calculation to encompass all other firms that have engaged in the same shoddy practices and to cover the entire history of recorded jazz since 1920—the mere contemplation of it is enough to make one's head swim (or one's heart ache).

Hence although Mark Levine's good fortune in securing a measure of recompense from United Artists is, to be sure, cause for rejoicing, the celebrating should be tempered by the realization that this is one very minor skirmish in a protracted conflict, one in which the great majority of the victories have gone not to the artists but to the corporations that exploit and defraud them. Nor should the relatively happy ending of Levine's tale blind us to the object lessons it has to teach. For if recording firms such as United Artists did not regard jazz musicians with barely concealed contempt—a contempt initially visited upon black artists, but now democratically expanded to take in those whites who perversely insist on following black models—they would not attempt to deprive those musicians of their lawful earnings with such deplorable persistence and regularity.

Finally, in addition to encouraging the heightened exploitation of the individual jazz artist, the contempt for black music that pervades white-business circles also operates to injure the music as a whole. That injury, which goes beyond the harm inflicted on any single performer, is the subject of chapter 4, directly below.

NOTES

1. See, for a few diverse examples, Francis Jennings's telling comments on the English ruling class's maltreatment of the Irish in the sixteenth and seventeenth centuries in *The Invasion of America: Indians, Colo-*

nialism, and the Cant of Conquest (New York: W.W. Norton, 1976), pp. 7, 45–46, 153; Edmund S. Morgan's revealing discussion of that same class's thinking on the related subjects of slavery and the poor, chapters 15 and 16 in *American Slavery, American Freedom: The Ordeal of Colonial Virginia* (New York: W.W. Norton, 1975); and David Brody's graphic account, in *Steelworkers in America: The Nonunion Era* (Cambridge, MA: Harvard University Press, 1960), of the way in which steel mill owners in the twentieth century ground the faces of the mass of Slavic and Italian workers as far into the dirt as circumstances would permit.

2. Jackie McLean quoted in A.B. Spellman, *Four Lives in the Bebop Business* (New York: Random House, 1966), pp. 213–14.

3. See Bob Porter's notes to the album *25 Years of Prestige* (Prestige P–24046).

4. *Ibid.*

5. All quotations about Lubinsky and Savoy Records are taken from Bob Porter's notes to *The Roots of Rock 'N' Roll* (Savoy SJL 2221).

6. I discuss this period of my life in the context of demonstrating why it is impossible for most would-be jazz critics to make a living at that trade in chapter 3 of the companion volume to this one, *John Coltrane and the Jazz Revolution of the 1960s* (New York: Pathfinder Press, 1998), the revised and expanded edition of *Black Nationalism and the Revolution in Music.*

7. Thiele quoted in Frank Kofsky, "The New Wave: Bob Thiele talks to Frank Kofsky about John Coltrane," *Coda*, May–June 1968, p. 10.

8. Quoted in *ibid.*, p. 3.

9. Quoted in *ibid.*, p. 6.

10. After a record producer chooses the instruments, song titles, and arrangements he plans to use in a session, part of the contractor's assignment is to hire the appropriate musicians.

11. Frank Kofsky, notes to *The Soul of Bonnie and Clyde* (ABC Bluesway 6018).

12. In Mark Levine's case, the statement to him from the Harry Fox Agency (as shown in Appendix B) reveals that UA wrongfully treated as "free" some 3,675 copies of *Saudade* sold during the first year after its release.

4

If you're black, get back:
double standards
in the recording industry

In the spheres of production and distribution, as in so many others, the position of the artist in capitalist society is unique, ambiguous and, above all, perilous in the extreme.

In contrast to the manual laborer, the artist, as I remarked in chapter 1, does own the tools of his or her trade. Unlike the skilled craftsman or artisan, however, the artist does not have complete control over the production and distribution processes; consequently, he or she is dependent on others. Hence where an automobile mechanic may be able to establish her own repair shop, a glazier his own stained glass works, or a baker his own bakery, very few painters or sculptors will possess their own galleries.

Analogously, very few jazz musicians control their own recording companies,* and fewer yet have any share in running

---

* To be sure, a number of jazz artists have established their own recording operations; but it is doubtful if all such artist-owned firms together account for one percent of the total number of jazz recordings released each year. For the recording industry as a whole, the importance of the artist-owned jazz recording firm is, naturally, more marginal still.

the nightclubs, festivals, and booking agencies on which most musicians rely for their survival. As a result, the way in which the white executives who do command these economic institutions regard black music in general and jazz in particular is of crucial significance for the well-being of the jazz artist. If these executives are favorably disposed toward jazz, then of necessity employment opportunities for jazz musicians will be relatively plentiful. If, conversely, these same executives are indifferent or antagonistic toward jazz, then the working jazz performer will find it that much more difficult to eke out a livelihood.

This concentration of power over the means of production and distribution gives the executive class almost unlimited control over the professional life of a jazz artist. Should such an artist happen to displease these executives, he or she will for all practical purposes cease to exist, at least so far as the public is concerned. At the dawn of the 1960s, for instance, singer Abbey Lincoln collaborated with Max Roach and others in recording a pair of powerful and explosive albums, *We Insist! The Freedom Now Suite* and *Straight Ahead*,[1] that excited a great deal of active hostility from the white Establishment in jazz; as a result, Abbey Lincoln's once-thriving career as a recording artist came to an abrupt halt. "I haven't been invited to record in this country" since the Candid discs were initially released, she told me sixteen years after that event.[2]

As easy as it is to stifle an individual voice, those who dominate the political economy of jazz find it hardly more difficult to silence an entire group of artists. As Abbey Lincoln pointedly observed in the same interview, "It's the recording industry—that's how much power those people have."[3] Indeed it is, and indeed they do. The vast and growing wealth and power of the recording industry vis-à-vis other entertainment media has been one of the most striking developments of the last few decades. From being the tail of the dog, the business of making and selling records has become the dog itself. Thus, where sales of soundtrack recordings were once ancillary to the production of motion pictures, those pictures often are concocted as a means of publicizing the records with which they are associated. Similarly, it is a commonplace that the leading popular music performers now embark on tours not because they want to perform in public, but rather to promote a recording whose release has been timed to coincide with the tour.

If this suggests that the recording industry has come to exert a predominant influence in determining the relative economic success or failure of a musical artist, the suggestion is well taken. From a theoretical standpoint, it is always possible that an artist may become popular even without extensive sales of his or her recordings. In practice, this happens about as often as objects spontaneously falling upward. There may be other paths to musical fame and fortune, but the tried-and-true approach consists of the following sequence: (1) recordings; (2) promotion by the recording company (or companies); (3) sizable and growing sales of the recordings; (4) another round of recordings and promotion. And so on, ad infinitum.

In this scheme of things, the recording firms hardly play the role of reluctant candidates patiently waiting to have greatness thrust upon them. On the contrary, as befits their lofty position in a sector of the economy that each year accounts for tens of billions of dollars in sales revenues, recording company executives do their utmost to insure that none of their investments will be disastrous and all of them, if possible, will be monumentally profitable. That is to say that, like their counterparts in other industries, executives in this one are implicated up to their eyebrows in what John Kenneth Galbraith has called "the management of specific demand."[4] The question of which recordings deserve to be made, distributed, and publicized, in other words, is entirely too important to be left to anything so dicey as the vagaries of public taste. Recording company executives as a group are neither saintly nor stupid; it can scarcely come as any surprise that they attempt to create and control consumer demand in every conceivable manner. Laissez-faire concepts may be all very well in introductory classes in economics, but the costs of production for recordings by some popular music artists and groups can easily run to millions of dollars. The mere possibility of not making profits of comparable size is sufficient to overcome any lingering attachment to laissez-faire ideology.

All of which means that executives in the recording industry possess not simply an immense amount of influence over the public's musical preferences, not just the power to make or break an individual artist, but even more than that, the wherewithal to determine whether a complete *body of music*—in this case, jazz—goes heard or unheard. Of even greater moment than the treatment of any single artist by the recording industry is the question of the reception of jazz as a whole by white executives within that industry. Denying an opportunity to a particular artist is, of course, a serious matter. But denying that same opportunity to an entire *group* of artists—that is a subject whose gravity beggars description.

To convey my meaning in concrete terms, I have compiled a list of some of the better known bebop-oriented jazz musicians who recorded frequently (often as leaders) during the late 1950s and/or early 1960s, but whose recording activity for U.S. firms* from the middle of the 1960s to the middle or end of the 1970s declined precipitously. The inventory is neither short nor lacking in names of the illustrious: Pepper Adams, Bob Brookmeyer, Ray Bryant, George Coleman, Junior Cook, Sonny Criss, Ted Curson, Walter Davis, Kenny Dorham, Kenny Drew, Art Farmer,

---

* Because my concern is with the recording industry in the United States—which does, after all, have preferential access to the largest single market of any place on earth—I am excluding consideration of albums made by some of these artists for European or Japanese firms. I am similarly disregarding albums containing music recorded earlier but released many years later, as these are even more misleading. Eric Dolphy, for instance, had a much greater number of records issued under his name during the 1970s and 1980s than he did prior to his death in 1964. Nonetheless, he was forced to be in Europe at the moment of his demise by the fact he was unable to find sufficient employment to survive in the land of his birth. If we were to go by the number of his recordings that became available in the decades after he died, however, we would conclude that his career never had appeared more promising!

Frank Foster, Red Garland, Dexter Gordon, Johnny Griffin, Jim Hall, Jimmy Heath, J.J. Johnson, Philly Joe Jones, Harold Land, Abbey Lincoln, Junior Mance, Charlie Mariano, Jackie McLean, Hank Mobley, Julian Priester, Max Roach, Lucky Thompson, Mal Waldron, and Mary Lou Williams. To this enumeration should be added the names of such post-bebop artists as Cecil Taylor, Ornette Coleman, Archie Shepp, Andrew Hill, and the many others who have gone years at a time without the release of an album of new material.

What I cannot emphasize too strongly in this context is that there are *no economic reasons whatsoever* why these artists have been refused the opportunity to have their music recorded and disseminated. The case of Dexter Gordon makes the point concisely. In 1977, after having been unaffiliated with a U.S. firm since his expatriation to Europe at the start of the 1960s, Gordon signed a contract with Columbia Records while continuing to make his home abroad. (Columbia later changed its name to CBS Records; later still, it was purchased by Sony and renamed accordingly.) The public response to the first few of Gordon's albums released by Columbia was overwhelmingly favorable. So why, then, did it take until 1977 for the saxophonist to be approached by Columbia? Why could he not have been signed by that corporation in 1970, say, or 1975? Answer: there was nothing at all preventing Gordon from having gone with Columbia years earlier. Certainly, his popularity after 1977 was not the result of any change in his style, the main outlines of which had been set since the late 1940s. But the two presidents of Columbia Records from 1967 to the mid-1970s, Clive Davis and Goddard Lieberson, simply did not care to record jazz musicians, a decision they rationalized by maintaining that there was no demand for the music. Their successor as president of the company, Bruce Lundvall, in contrast, was convinced that there was a market for unadulterated bebop and therefore made Gordon an acceptable offer. The matter is as simple and straightforward as that.

What is significant is that in each instance the Columbia executive bureaucracy was able to manipulate matters in such a way as to bear out its preconceptions about the extent of consumer interest in jazz recordings. Both Davis and Lieberson were, to put it mildly, ill-disposed toward jazz, added few jazz artists to Columbia's roster, expended next to nothing advertising jazz recordings—and thus brought about a situation that supported their pessimistic appraisal of the market for jazz discs. Lundvall, however, chose to put the corporation's vast public-relations prowess behind Gordon's Columbia albums, thereby virtually guaranteeing that they would sell well and justify his initial decision to recruit the saxophonist. Hence regardless of whether they favored or opposed Columbia's involvement with jazz, the company's upper-echelon executives were able to use its prodigious resources to produce economic results to provide seemingly objective and irrefutable "proof" of the correctness of their views.

To generalize from this representative example, what is crucial in determining whether a corporate giant such as Columbia will record, issue, and publicize works by jazz artists is least of all the existing economic conditions, for the firm's ability to *create* demand is sufficient to overcome all but the most cataclysmic circumstances. Hence in reality, rather than first analyzing consumer demand and then deciding how much jazz recording activity it will undertake, it is more nearly the case that once a company the size of Columbia has reached such a decision, it can generate a level of demand capable of absorbing the number of recordings it chooses to release.

With that in mind, let us turn to an examination of this chapter's central concern: how *do* recording company executives decide what kinds of music will (and will not) be recorded, in what quantities, and with what amounts budgeted for promotion? This is a pivotal question in any analysis of the political economy of jazz because, when all is said and done, the fate of entire genres of music—not to mention that of the artists who create them—rests on the outcome of such decisions. And although estimates of potential profits and losses, to be sure, influence the decisions, those estimates are not, in and of themselves, what determine the final outcome.

For our purposes it suffices to investigate the way in which the topmost stratum of executives at a single firm, Columbia Records, has approached jazz. Nothing is lost by way of universality in restricting ourselves to this one corporation, because Columbia's immense size and wealth make it the bellwether of the industry. When Columbia executives choose to expand the scale of their jazz-recording activities, heads of other companies feel secure in doing likewise, confident in the knowledge that the massive outlays Columbia can expend on advertising will have spillover effects that benefit them as well. Conversely, when Columbia sees fit to retrench on its production of jazz albums, other companies will be quick to do the same. It is hardly surprising, therefore, that those periods in which Columbia issued jazz recordings in quantity—the years 1957 to 1965, for instance—were ones of comparative prosperity for jazz musicians, while those in which its involvement with jazz was reduced (1967 to 1976, say) were far more lean by comparison.

No sooner do we begin our inquiry into the attitudes of Columbia executives regarding jazz than we again confront the figure of John Hammond, whom we earlier met in chapter 2 in surveying the history of the heightened exploitation of jazz artists by white-owned corporations. Hammond spent several decades with Columbia, retiring in 1975 as the director of talent acquisition, a position he had held since the close of the 1950s. In June of 1969, he attended a three-day conference on Black Music in College and University Curricula at Indiana University, the proceedings of which were captured on tape, transcribed, and later published as part of a book, *Black Music in Our Culture*.[5] Hammond's comments there, it will soon be clear, are invaluable for understanding how senior recording company executives view jazz and other forms of black music.

The participants at the conference lost little time in getting to the heart of the matter with Hammond. The first question put to him directly after his typically self-aggrandizing summary of his career was, "What avant garde jazz is Columbia Records engaged in recording now?"[6] Hammond's answer, a characteristically skillful blend of evasions, distortions, and quar-ter-truths, is virtually impossible to paraphrase. To convey the full flavor, therefore, I will quote the bulk of it, then subject it to scrutiny bit by bit.

With his two opening sentences, Hammond immediately sought to position himself on the side of the angels: "I'm re-cording [saxophonist] Archie Shepp and [drummer] Sonny [*sic*] Murray on Monday. We ought to have a lot of fun." Assuming that Hammond's recording session with Shepp and Sunny Mur-ray actually took place—which is by no means certain—surely after nearly thirty years have elapsed it is not impermissible to ask: when are the results going to be made available? But, of course, it is well within the bounds of possibility that no such recording session was ever planned, much less held. For one thing, neither Shepp's name nor Murray's appears in the index to Hammond's autobiography, nor is there any mention of a recording session with these artists in the "Selective Discogra-phy" included in that volume.[7] For another, Hammond, as I will show momentarily, was himself implacably hostile to the type of music Shepp and Murray then played. Accordingly, we prob-ably should view Hammond's statement about a recording ses-sion with Shepp and Murray as a ploy—analogous to observ-ing that some of one's best friends are colored—intended to get him off the hook by showing that where the jazz revolution of the 1960s was concerned, his heart was in the right place. Thus, the executive continued in a similar vein:

> Although I'm director of talent acquisitions and an executive producer at Columbia, I do not make the final decisions. . . . [I]n this specialized field of pure jazz . . . the possibility of an enormous profit . . . is minimal, even with the biggest artists like Miles Davis and Thelonious Monk. The records may only break even. I've been recording with Sonny [*sic*] Murray,* and

---

* Note the second reference to Sunny Murray—again, however, with no spe-cific information about titles, albums to be released, or anything else.

you know the business will hesitate to make concessions when numbers might last eighteen minutes and might not even get much airplay, even in the underground. I'm sorry we've never recorded Cecil Taylor. He is a genius, but he is being recorded. Archie Shepp is under contract to Impulse. Albert Ayler and a lot of those guys are being recorded. One of the problems is that Columbia is a huge operation. We need to sell about 15,000 copies a year of a recording with the accounting system we have, the money it costs to package the thing [and so on].[8]

Following that deluge of exculpations, equivocations, and outright falsehoods, a few factual corrections may come as a breath of fresh air.

Item 1: No doubt Cecil Taylor is "a genius," but, Hammond's assertion notwithstanding, he was not "being recorded" in 1969, had not been recorded for three years—his entire output for the 1960s numbered fewer than half a dozen discs—and would not have a new album issued by an American company of even moderate size until the middle of the 1970s. As was also the case in his fictionalized account of the death of Bessie Smith (recounted in chapter 2), Hammond either knew the truth about Taylor's recording activity or could have learned it in a matter of minutes with one or two well-placed telephone calls. As was again the case with the circumstances of Bessie Smith's death, any ignorance on Hammond's part was hardly inadvertent. If nothing else, it enabled him to parry a potentially embarrassing question in front of an audience of educators evidently anxious about the reception being afforded the newest innovations in jazz by the country's largest producer of phonograph records.

Item 2: No one with whom I have spoken or corresponded and no analysis I have read supports Hammond's contention that Columbia or any other record company "need[s] to sell about 15,000 copies *a year* of a recording [my italics]" in order to show a profit. On the contrary, the evidence suggests that most jazz albums begin to earn profits as soon as they reach sales on the order of two thousand copies for a medium-sized firm, five to seven thousand copies for a larger one. But regardless of whether a jazz recording starts to become profitable after two, five, or seven thousand copies have been sold, even the largest of these amounts is still a far cry from the 15,000 copies that Hammond claimed was the minimal *annual* sales figure acceptable to Columbia's executives.[9]

Item 3: What is more, conclusive evidence that Hammond was deliberately misleading his audience can be obtained from an unimpeachable source—Columbia Records itself. In 1951, that firm brought out four long-playing albums of performances by Bessie Smith. According to Chris Albertson, "This fine series was a slow but steady seller which the company kept in its catalogue for nineteen years," until it was deleted to make way for the new Bessie Smith reissue recordings Columbia released in the 1970s. During the nineteen years they were in print (roughly the same years that Hammond worked at Columbia), Albertson informs us, these four albums sold a *total* of about 20,000 copies—or, on the average, slightly fewer than 300 copies per album per year.[10] If Hammond were still alive, it would be most enlightening to have him explain what ever became of the sales figure of "15,000 copies a year of a recording" with which he attempted to mystify his listeners at the Indiana University conference on black music. Even he would have to agree, would he not, that 300 copies per annum is a considerable distance from 15,000?

Item 4: But perhaps the "15,000 copies a year of a recording" that Hammond invoked so quickly is merely an *average* that applies to Columbia's overall operations but not to each and every recording released on that label. Hammond, naturally, isn't notably lucid on this point—when your aim is to befuddle your hearers, clarity is not the most probable outcome. Still, inasmuch as Columbia's most popular albums sell hundreds of thousands (and in some instances, even millions) of copies apiece, if the "15,000 copies a year" is an average, as opposed to an individual, criterion, there is no reason it cannot be attained by allowing the greater sales of popular records to compensate for the lesser sales of jazz records. For that matter, if the "15,000 copies a year of a recording" is interpreted in this sense, it should even be possible for Columbia to release jazz albums that do not even recover their full costs of production.

Such a line of reasoning was in fact endorsed by Hammond's boss, Clive Davis, who was the head of Columbia Records from 1967 until he was discharged in the spring of 1973 and "served with the company's civil complaint against me, alleging ninety-four thousand dollars' worth of expense-account violations during my six years as President."[11] Davis's words on this score are completely unambiguous: "Everything *doesn't* have to pay for itself. But if you are willing to release albums that lose money, you should either balance them with profitable ones or believe that the loss was worth taking for the sake of the music."[12]

Given the testimony of Columbia's former president that "everything *doesn't* have to pay for itself," there should be no obstacle to that company's issuing jazz albums that sell fewer than "15,000 copies a year." The only problem is that such an enlightened policy of corporate noblesse oblige was not devised to benefit art music created in the African-American tradition, but to support music composed in the European symphonic ("classical") idiom. What is more, such a flagrant double standard—subsidies for European concert music, pay-your-own-way for jazz—was enthusiastically defended by that great patron of black music, John Hammond. At the same Indiana University conference on black music in 1969 from which I have already quoted some of his remarks, Hammond declared his allegiance to this double standard in terms that leave no room for misunderstanding. "Once in a while," he explained,

Columbia will undertake something like the recording of all of [Anton von] Webern's works. This may have sold three or four thousand copies, and the company may have lost up to $30,000 on the venture, *yet they make up for it with the popular hits that come out* [my italics].[13]

Though Hammond on this occasion claimed that such losses are sustained only "once in a while," another of his statements at the Indiana University conference makes it unmistakably plain that *deficits incurred in the production of recordings of European symphonic music are a regular and predictable aspect of Columbia's operation.* In his own words:

> Now you know if we sell 20,000 copies at retail of, say, a [Gustav] Mahler symphony conducted by [Leonard] Bernstein, we think we're doing pretty well, *even though 20,000 sales doesn't pay a quarter of the cost* [my italics].[14]

A pity that none of Hammond's listeners thought to demand to know how he and Columbia Records could react with such equanimity to losses of tens of thousands of dollars on symphonic works by Webern and Mahler while still insisting that every single jazz recording sell "15,000 copies a year." It would have been most edifying, one may be sure, to hear his attempts to contrive a plausible answer to *that* query.

To give the devil his due, the double standard articulated so plainly by Hammond—hundreds of thousands of dollars to subsidize the recording of European symphonies, not one cent for jazz—is not original with him. On the contrary, in defending it, he was, one supposes, merely "doing his job" as an upper-level executive of, and prominent spokesman for, Columbia Records. That much emerges from the remarks of former Columbia president Clive Davis:

> Obviously, not every decision was determined by profit-and-loss consideration. We willingly *lost* money on Vladimir Horowitz. Each of his albums cost Columbia in guaranty, recording and advertising expenses about a hundred thousand dollars; they generally recouped half that amount. But it *was*

Horowitz. . . . We decided that the business loss was more than offset by the musical contribution and the accompanying prestige.[15]

And again:

Now it costs from twenty-five to fifty thousand dollars to record a classical album. The losses on this can range from minor to substantial, especially if you add in advertising outlays. [Recordings by certain symphony orchestras] generally sold well over a long period of time; so you couldn't compute your profit-loss ratio in the first or second year. . . . Yet, even if sales were calculated over a five- to ten-year period, most classical recordings failed to recoup their recording costs.[16]

If only corporate executives at the rank of Clive Davis and John Hammond were so graciously resigned to accepting financial losses from the production, promotion, and distribution of jazz recordings!*

But, of course, they are not. Nor does it take a great deal of abstruse thought to discover why. For businessmen of the Davis and Hammond variety, the symphonic music of Europe is, as Davis's comments about Vladimir Horowitz quoted immediately above explicitly acknowledge, a matter of infinite prestige. Only a philistine, therefore, would be so gauche as to soil something that sublime by mentioning fiscal considerations in the same breath.

Jazz, in contrast, as we have been informed all too many times, is nigger music. Oh, to be sure, it isn't played in whorehouses any more, and now there are some white misfits who also are involved in it. But when push comes to shove, it is *still* nigger

---

* To make my position unambiguously clear, I have no objection to subsidizing the recording of works by Gustav Mahler—indeed, it is not uncommon for me to make a 120-mile round trip for the pleasure of seeing one of his symphonies performed. All I ask is that the same largesse be showered on African-American music of comparable weight and quality.

music, and never mind if some of the niggers happen to be white. Subsidize nigger music? What an absurd notion! (Perhaps it is relevant at this point to remind the reader of chapter 3's discussion of the racist contempt for black music consistently exhibited by white recording company executives.)

Also related to the question of subsidies is a different aspect of the double standard for symphonic versus jazz artists that comes into play when sales of recordings begin to decline. In the case of the symphonic artist, the unprofitability has more or less been anticipated all along—witness the remarks by Clive Davis on Vladimir Horowitz—and thus can be greeted with a philosophical shrug of the shoulders and some offhand comments about art, culture, the cosmos, and the like, should it actually materialize. But if the sales of a *jazz musician's* albums begin to show signs of slipping, then, my friends, it is time to storm heaven and earth. Only by keeping this fact in mind can we understand the unrelenting pressure that former Columbia president Clive Davis applied to Columbia jazz artist Miles Davis in striving to convince the latter to play jazz-rock, appear at the Fillmore East and "other rock halls around the country," go on tour with the popular music group Santana, and so forth.[17] To the degree that the morass into which jazz sunk during much of the 1970s and 1980s was an outgrowth of Miles Davis's earliest steps in this direction at the end of the 1960's, a considerable share of the responsibility for this lovely state of affairs, too, can be laid at the door of the executive Mr. Davis.*

What needs underscoring in this connection is that the head of Columbia Records would have reacted in a drastically different fashion had it been Vladimir Horowitz rather than Miles Davis whose record sales were dwindling. Can you imagine him urging Horowitz to perform at the Fillmore East, play on the same bill as Santana, and the like, in order to boost the sales

---

* As is evident from his exultation over the decision of pianist Herbie Hancock to align himself with the camp of jazz fusion; Davis's ecstatic account of Hancock's conversion is in Clive Davis and James Willwerth, *Clive: Inside the Record Busi-*

of his recordings? If that suggestion would be regarded as obscene when tendered to the pianist, why should it be thought any more appropriate when made to an influential and creative jazz musician? Could the answer be, because European symphonic music is Art-with-a-capital-A, whereas jazz is . . . you-know-what?

In light of such attitudes towards black music, no wonder that the leading innovators in jazz during the 1960s found conditions at Columbia Records anything but hospitable. The hostility to the new developments of that decade, moreover, was as fully shared by John Hammond as by any of his colleagues at Columbia, his carefully crafted image as the altruistic benefactor of black music and musicians notwithstanding. Thus when he was safely out of earshot of the participants at the 1969 Indiana University conference on black music, he permitted himself the indulgence of expressing his actual feelings about the kind of music performed by Archie Shepp, Cecil Taylor, Albert Ayler, et alia:

ness (New York: Ballantine Books, 1976), p. 165. Note further that drummer Max Roach's experience with Atlantic Records is very similar in this regard to that of Miles Davis at Columbia. "During the early '70s," Roach has related,

> I was called into Atlantic and it was suggested to me that I do some material that was familiar to the world, *for sales* [my italics]. It was suggested in such a subtle way. Nesuhi Ertegun [Atlantic vice president] said, "Max, we've been knowing each other for years and you should really be rich." . . . So I said, "Yeah, I couldn't agree more, but how do I go about it, Nesuhi?" And he proceeds to tell me that you piggyback, coattail on different songs, basically you do familiar material. So I went home and called him and said, "Well, I'll do Negro spirituals, which is familiar material." Of course, I missed the boat. That was the last record I did for them.
>
> During that time was the beginning of fusion and crossover, the styles that prevail today. When I read Clive Davis' book, Miles [Davis] was asked to do the same thing.

Roach's testimony demonstrates that efforts at pushing jazz musicians into playing fusion and crossover styles were an industry-wide phenomenon, not merely the idiosyncratic whim of one or another recording company executive. See Bert Primack, "Max Roach: There's No Stoppin' the Professor from Boppin'," *down beat*, November 2, 1978, p. 21.

What they're putting down really doesn't make that much sense to me. When you throw out tonality and certain disciplines, you're left with not enough. A record supervisor is not really in control of a session like that. . . . You just have to give the musicians their heads.[18]

And if there is one thing on which John Hammond insists where black musicians are concerned, it is, as we observed in chapter 3, that he must be "really in control." But if nothing else, this statement should suffice to explain why the recording session with Archie Shepp and Sunny Murray that Hammond claimed to be producing in 1969 has never yet seen the light of day.

Given that Hammond's sentiments are those of a man who professes himself a lover of jazz, we can readily understand why few jazz artists, and still fewer of the most-recent innovators, were allowed to affiliate with Columbia Records from the middle of the 1960s to the late 1970s. And among those who were signed to contracts with that firm during this period, no one's treatment more clearly reflected the double standard for European symphonic art and Afro-American art than that of Ornette Coleman.

Toward the close of the 1960s, Columbia began to come under fire, particularly from Miles Davis, for its failure to bring more black jazz artists onto its roster. (With Paul Winter, Denny Zeitlin, Friedrich Gulda, Clare Fischer, Dave Brubeck, Don Ellis, Bill Evans and others all represented on Columbia albums from the mid–1960s on, it had no shortage of white jazz performers.) As Clive Davis himself acknowledged, Miles Davis "poked at the company in press interviews," referring to himself as "the company nigger" and "complain[ing] in *Ebony* or *Jet* that Columbia didn't have enough 'really black' artists."[19]

These charges, implicitly threatening to affect the sales of Columbia records, evidently stung Clive Davis, for he later conceded that they were "probably true at the time—but I was hardly pleased to have the problem aired."[20] In all likelihood, therefore, it was such criticism that prompted Columbia to make an offer to Ornette Coleman. It does not appear that Columbia's executive had any genuine desire to record Coleman's music—his name, for instance, does not appear in the index to either Clive Davis's or John Hammond's autobiography—but they must have hoped that having him at Columbia would mute most of the attacks leveled at the firm by Miles Davis and others.

During his brief tenure with Columbia, the company issued two albums of Ornette Coleman's music: one, *Science Fiction*, is a collection of eight improvisations by small jazz groups; the other, *The Skies of America*, is an ambitious work by Coleman for himself and the London Symphony Orchestra.[21] Neither album was advertised even modestly, with the predictable result that both promptly dropped from sight shortly after their release early in the 1970s. In this way, Columbia's management was in the position of having killed two birds with the proverbial one stone. First, signing Coleman to a contract with the company succeeded in stilling the protests over Columbia's lack of black artists. Second, the failure of Coleman's discs to sell in immense quantities—a hardly unexpected outcome, given Columbia's unwillingness to promote them—handed the company's executives a potent weapon they could brandish against present and future critics: "We told you so!" By never wavering in their conviction that Coleman's efforts at Columbia would, from the standpoint of sales, come to naught, the firm's intrepid officers were able to bring about precisely that result.

This arrangement seems to have served its purposes exceedingly well for all of the principals save one—Ornette Coleman himself. Subsequently, he was willing to unburden himself to a sympathetic reporter, and his testimony comprises a veritable textbook on the operation of the double standard for symphonic *versus* jazz artists at Columbia.

"I'm so pissed-off with Columbia" was how Coleman began relating his experiences at that company. "I was put in the situation where they're supposed to be humanitarians," he continued,

aware of everything that's going on. *But I didn't get the same interest in my music as [New York Philharmonic conductor Pierre] Boulez did recording someone else's music [my italics].* I didn't even get all of it on the record [*Skies of America*], only 40 minutes. The budget that Boulez could get for recording a Bartok piece—the rehearsal money—would have allowed me to finish [recording] my whole piece. I could've done my record exactly as I wanted to do it, and if it didn't sell, I still would have the privilege of knowing they were *with* me.[22]

But *with* Coleman, it appears, is evidently the last place that Columbia's white managers wished to be found.

The sole satisfaction left to Coleman was that of understanding exactly what was taking place at Columbia, and why: "Instead of the concept of music for the purpose of people," he observed pointedly,

it has become a judgment stick for people's politics. . . . The white people have created values, and they've created categories to identify their own class structure in the way they want, or to decide what is good enough to be in their presence. Just like the record man says, "We don't have nowhere to classify you—we know you're black." Like on *Skies of America:* "Now if you put in titles [on the sections of the piece], that'll give you lots of air play—you'll be really cool."

Coleman's conclusion was as wistful as it was to the point: "To me, there should be a human politics."

Ornette Coleman's unhappy and frustrating ordeal at Columbia, though important in its own right, is not our main concern here. Rather, the significance of his account is that it provides us with a diagrammatic illustration of the double standard that prevails at the highest levels of the recording industry: financial support for European symphonic music as a matter of course, nothing whatsoever for Afro-American art music, call it what you will.

This double standard, in turn, is one component of a system

of assumptions and procedures that oppresses both jazz and the musicians who originate it. Corporations such as Columbia neither expect nor require European symphonic music to be profitable, and therefore will continue to produce recordings of symphonic music regardless of the quantities in which they sell. For jazz, however, no such guarantee exists. When recording company executives happen to believe, for one reason or another, that issuing jazz albums *will* be profitable, then more of them will indeed be issued, they will be promoted with substantial advertising budgets and, in consequence, generally will sell well. So far, so good. But should such executives instead conclude that returns from the sales of jazz discs are not sufficient to justify the expenditures their production entails, then both the number of jazz recordings released and the number sold will go into a steep decline.

Far more often than not, recording company executives subscribe to the latter belief rather than the former. Viewing jazz as a thing that, unlike European symphonic music, has little intrinsic merit and bestows nothing in the way of prestige on those associated with it, they see no reason to be concerned about its fate, as the treatment of Ornette Coleman at Columbia illustrates only too graphically. If at any given moment jazz miraculously manages to flourish unaided, fine; the executives will not be averse to accepting whatever profits from the music they can steer in their direction. But if jazz should prove in need of assistance in order to survive and be propagated—tough luck! Do not hold your breath waiting for that assistance to arrive.

In practice, then, these attitudes—which are merely the expression of the standard themes of white supremacy translated into the realm of music—have the effect of retarding the development of jazz and adding to the problems of un- and underemployment confronting the jazz artist. As long as jazz is perceived by white recording company managers as the second-class music of second-class people, so long will this situation continue to exist.

Confirmation of the correctness of this diagnosis comes from an individual who acquired firsthand knowledge of conditions inside the recording industry from his employment as "the jazz publicist for CBS [Columbia] Records" late in the 1970s. Even the title of Peter Keepnews's article, "Why Big Record Companies Let Jazz Down,"[23] is revealing; portions of his testimony, moreover, provide decisive support for the argument I set forth above.

At the time Columbia hired him, Keepnews believed that the firm had decided to devote some of its immense financial and organizational resources to jazz; this quaint notion, however, did not long survive:

> There are some people who will still argue that CBS did make that choice and continues to be sincerely committed to jazz, but after having spent two years there[,] I am not one of them. . . . There is, as I learned rather quickly, a substantial difference between putting records out and selling them. And to simply record and release jazz records does not necessarily represent a sincere commitment to anything.

Even worse, as the case of Ornette Coleman earlier demonstrated, recording and releasing albums by jazz artists without supplying the kind of promotion that would cause them to sell in the end probably does the careers of those artists more harm than good.

Once at Columbia, Keepnews rapidly learned that although the president of the company, Bruce Lundvall, was himself a lover of jazz, the remainder of the bureaucracy—just as everything in this chapter heretofore would predict—was implacably hostile to it. Because "there is very little that one person, even if he's the president, can accomplish in an organization that size without the support of his subordinates," Lundvall's good intentions for jazz ultimately came to naught.

Of the most celebrated—and most misunderstood—action that Columbia's chief executive took in the field of jazz, for instance, Keepnews writes:

It didn't take me long to discover that Lundvall's signing of Dexter Gordon had been barely tolerated by many key people in the company, and that his subsequent jazz signings were provoking a definite backlash. There was a deep-seated belief that . . . jazz records, no matter how ostensibly "commercial," could not sell.

To an extent, that belief amounts to a self-fulfilling prophecy—*if you don't work a jazz album, it won't sell* [my italics].

Self-fulfilling prophecy or no, however, Columbia's officers were bent on sabotaging any policy even moderately favorable to jazz. So potent was their antipathy that

what the CBS Records field office ended up doing was, in effect, ignoring the jazz product [recordings]—devoting as little attention to it as possible. *In many cases, new jazz albums never even made their way into the important record stores in major cities* [my italics].

Columbia's officers were in this way able to demonstrate that jazz is an abomination, an albatross from which the company should cut itself loose at the earliest possible moment. This opposition to jazz supposedly was based on hardheaded economic logic, but, as Keepnews observes, management's reasoning began by assuming exactly what it was seeking to prove—that jazz recordings are intrinsically unsalable. In reality, therefore, the "economic" argument was nothing more than a figleaf, dragged in to lend a modicum of respectability to what was in fact a thoroughly racist outlook. As I have remarked more than once in this chapter, executives at recording companies such as Columbia operate on the basis of a cultural double standard that denies black art music—that is, jazz—the kind of financial backing that European art music routinely receives.

Furthermore, Keepnews's words make it plain that black music of *any* variety was tolerated at Columbia only to the extent that it could sell records:

The jazz/progressive area was officially part of the company's black music marketing department, which meant in effect—although nobody ever said it in so many words—that the white people in the company tended to look on jazz as a "black" concern and not something they had to deal with. But the thrust of the black music marketing department was in the area of R&B [rhythm and blues] and disco—the music that gets played on black radio. That, of course, includes little if any "pure" jazz.

Thus, by relegating jazz to the "black music marketing department" and by insisting that this department be concerned solely about the profitability of whatever "product" it "marketed," Columbia's top executives were able to ensure that jazz at the company was fated for a certain, speedy, and unspectacular descent into oblivion. We can be positive that the members of Columbia's black music marketing division were only too aware of the contempt in which their white superiors held jazz.

As I noted earlier, a company policy of discriminating in favor of white art music and against black can scarcely be stated openly, but instead must be couched in "economic" terms. For that reason, Columbia's executives simply ignored the inconvenient fact that the company's recordings of symphonic music and opera sell at a loss, meanwhile maintaining that, as Keepnews puts it, "their job is not to help spread the word about jazz or to aid in the preservation of good art. Their job is to get hit records" (a viewpoint that, according to this author, "would appear to be here to stay"). "Right now," he continues, "there is a lot of product, but the prevailing attitude is that anything that doesn't look like a potential million-seller"—and few jazz albums fall into that category—"gets extremely short shrift." This assertion will no doubt come as a revelation in Columbia's symphonic division, which has *never* been required to turn a profit on any of its "product." But that is just the point: one set of rules for white art, rather a different set for black. At any rate, through such pseudoeconomic rationalizations the jazz artist at Columbia, as we have witnessed, is kept in a state of limbo, with no segment of the corporate bureaucracy responsible for the well-being of him or his music.

Whatever their other traits, jazz performers are rarely lacking in intelligence. It was but a short time before many of those contracted to Columbia surmised that "the only way to get the company to take an interest in them was to do their damnedest to make what they considered 'commercial,' 'black' albums." (The identification of "black" with "commercial" in Keepnews's sentence speaks volumes about the prevailing mentality at Columbia.) The outcome of these attempts is revealing: according to Keepnews, some jazz artists began

> trying to second-guess the needs of the label and, in many cases, coming up with albums that were neither artistically nor commercially very worthwhile. Other artists . . . tried to walk a tightrope between their artistic needs and what they saw as the need to get on the radio. But in almost all cases, the results were the same: The company paid little attention.

How otherwise? Jazz had repeatedly demonstrated its suitability for second-class citizenship at Columbia. From an artistic standpoint, it was axiomatic that jazz could never be considered the cultural equivalent of European art music. From the standpoint of profitability, there were several other types of black music that produced more revenue for the firm. Is it any wonder, then, that Columbia's management was indecently eager to see jazz dead and buried in its grave?

Some of Keepnews's conclusions are as germane to this chapter's thesis as his observations. He is at pains to disabuse his readers of the illusion to which "a lot of jazz musicians" subscribe—namely, "that if they sign with a major label, they will be treated with the respect they deserve and brought to a level of sales and public recognition that has long been denied them." Reviewing his two years at Columbia, Keepnews is forced to concede that although the "essence" of his job ostensibly was "to help these artists get greater recognition . . . in the long run, my job was a joke, as is CBS Records's commitment"—a word that should here appear in quotation marks—"to jazz."

"A lot is said about the cultural obligation of record companies to record jazz," Keepnews remarks in his final paragraph. "In principle," he continues,

> I don't disagree. But the fact is that the record business is not just a business but a *big* business, and to the extent that it has a sense of cultural obligation, it is an extremely small one.

To which one need only add: particularly when the culture in question exhibits the poor taste and dubious judgment to insist on parading its African-American antecedents for all to see.

NOTES

1. Max Roach, *We Insist! The Freedom Now Suite* (Candid 8002); Abbey Lincoln, *Straight Ahead* (Candid 8015).

2. Abbey Lincoln quoted in Frank Kofsky, "Abbey Lincoln," *Radio Free Jazz*, February 1977, p. 14.

3. Quoted in *ibid*.

4. That is the title of chapter 18 in John Kenneth Galbraith's study *The New Industrial State* (Boston: Houghton Mifflin, 1967).

5. Dominique-René de Lerma, ed., *Black Music in Our Culture: Curricular Ideas on the Subjects, Materials and Problems* (Kent, Ohio: Kent State University Press, 1970).

6. Quoted in *ibid.*, p. 54

7. See John Hammond and Irving Townsend, *John Hammond on Record* (New York: Ridge Press/Summit Books, 1977), pp. 412, 415, 416.

8. *Ibid.*

9. A detailed calculation of the "break-even point" at which the sales of a jazz album just suffices to recover the costs of production is included in my 1973 doctoral dissertation in history at the University of Pittsburgh, "Black Nationalism and the Revolution in Music: Social Forces

and Stylistic Change in the Music of John Coltrane and Others, 1954–1967," pp. 385–89. The sources I employed for that calculation are: Richard Nicholls, "Where Your $5.98 Goes," *Rock, 14* December 1970, p. 21; Bob Koester, "The Record Producer: A Dollars and Cents Analysis," *Coda*, March 1967, pp. 2–5; a letter from Koester to the author, May 13, 1971; a telephone interview with Koester, April 25, 1973; Francis Newton [E. J. Hobsbawm], *The Jazz Scene* (Harmondsworth, Middlesex: Penguin Books, 1961), pp. 172–73, notes A, B. In his letter to me of May 13, 1971, for instance, Bob Koester, himself the owner of a recording company (Delmark Records), states: "I don't think they [Columbia Records] require 15K [15,000 sales per annum], tho[ugh]. I guess that 5K would keep an album in print until they ran out of paper (Covers and Liners)." Koester likewise estimates the initial pressing of a Columbia jazz record at 10,000 copies. In a telephone interview on September 21, 1978, Pat Britt, who produced the majority of jazz recordings released on the Catalyst label, supplied a figure of eighty-five cents as the unit cost to the company of an album. Using the numbers given by Koester and Britt and bearing in mind that records are usually sold to the distributor by the manufacturer at twice the cost of production, it follows that Columbia would realize a profit on an initial pressing of 10,000 copies after 8,500 had been sold. If the original run were smaller, of course, the break-even point would be correspondingly lower. A first pressing of 5,000 copies, for example, would need sales of only 4,250 copies to recoup production expenditures.

10. See Chris Albertson, *Bessie* (New York: Stein and Day, 1972), p. 232.

11. Clive Davis and James Willwerth, *Clive: Inside the Record Business* (New York: Ballantine Books, 1976), p. 325.

12. *Ibid.*, p. 282

13. Quoted in *Black Music in Our Culture*, p. 115.

14. Quoted in *ibid.*, p. 113.

15. *Clive*, p. 272.

16. *Ibid.*, p. 267.

17. See *Clive*, pp. 299–303; the quotation is from p. 301.

18. Hammond's remarks are quoted in John McDonough, "John Hammond: Man for All Seasons," *down beat*, March 4, 1971, p. 13. Both this typically laudatory title and the equally flattering portrait that follows are the inevitable result of taking the executive's lavish self-praise at face value. Interestingly enough, though, Hammond's position on the

new forms of jazz in the 1960s was essentially a reiteration of his response to the bebop revolution of the 1940s: "To me, bebop is a collection of nauseating clichés, repeated *ad infinitum*"; Hammond is quoted in Ross Russell, *Bird Lives!: The High Life and Hard Times of Charlie (Yardbird) Parker* (New York: Charterhouse, 1973), p. 173.

19. *Clive*, p. 301.

20. *Ibid.*

21. See Ornette Coleman, *Science Fiction* (Columbia KC 31061) and *The Skies of America* (Columbia KC 31562).

22. This and the following quotation are in Michael Bourne, "Ornette's Interview," *down beat*, November 22, 1973, p. 17.

23. Peter Keepnews, "Why Big Record Companies Let Jazz Down," *Jazz Magazine*, vol. 4, no. 1 (1980), pp. 60–64.

Part 2

Approaching jazz history

5

You don't have to be intellectually dishonest
to defend the status quo in jazz—but it helps

April 27, 1977

To the Editors:
  I am afraid I can no longer tolerate professional association
with a supposedly scholarly journal that traffics in the embar-
rassing and wholly self-serving likes of Frank Kofsky's "Elvin
*Jones" (*Journal of Jazz Studies, Fall 1976). *This article—which*
despite my [name's] presence on the Journal's *masthead, ap-*
peared without my foreknowledge—brings to crisis a number
of questions concerning the intentions and professional quali-
fications of the Journal's *current editors, whose continuing over-*
emphasis upon sociology and social history (even on topics of
doubtful relevance to jazz) has evidently reached the point of
indiscrimination and disregard for documented fact.
  Please consider my resignation as editorial assistant effec-
tive immediately.

> *J.R. Taylor*
> Jazz Program
> SMITHSONIAN INSTITUTION
> WASHINGTON, D.C.[1]

No analysis of the white control of the black music of jazz would be complete without discussion of the two ways in which that control is exerted in the realm of ideas. First, in the three-quarters of a century of the music's existence, all but a handful of those who have written books, articles, and even advertisements about it, as well as those who have owned and edited the periodicals and published the volumes that have dealt with it, have been white men. Second and related, a great deal of this literature has served to deny, obscure, rationalize, or otherwise defend the single most glaring inequity connected with the production of the music: that black artistry has created it while white ownership has profited disproportionately from it.

To take these facets of white control in order, I do not subscribe to any dogma favoring skin-color fetishism. Being markedly pale in complexion myself, I could hardly be thought to look with approval on the notion that each and every white writer is necessarily an apologist for the kind of victimization of the jazz artist and discrimination against jazz music that I have outlined in previous chapters. Yet the truth of the matter is that, apart from a few scholarly musicologists and anthropologists whose research is primarily technical in nature, few if any of the best-known professional writers currently active in the United States are completely honest and objective in their treatment of the central social issue of jazz: black music *versus* white control.

Nor is it difficult to see why this is so. Almost without exception, authors whose livelihood comes from writing on jazz are dependent in myriad ways upon white executives for favors both large and small. Such favors run the gamut from fees of several hundred dollars to annotate albums for recording companies and programs for festivals and concerts to receiving free records and admission to nightclubs, concerts, and other performances; from having one's expenses paid for an evening on the town or a weekend at a festival to hearing the latest gossip within the industry while it is still fresh and spicy; from attending recording sessions to meeting (and perhaps even spending time with) artists one has long admired from afar. Whatever the specifics, the point is that writers find it enormously useful to be on the friendliest of terms with the leading jazz entrepreneurs and business executives.[2] And this, in turn, virtually guarantees that most white writers on jazz will prefer to conceal certain embarrassing truths, proclaim the virtues of an unjust status quo, and dismiss the complaints of black artists rather than risk incurring the wrath of those in possession of the power and influence to impede their careers.*

Thus, to take one flagrant example, Leonard Feather spills gallons of ink in his essay on "Jazz in the American Society," in *The New Edition of the Encyclopedia of Jazz*, striving to refute the argument that "jazz, as the property of the Negro, can only be played by whites to the extent that they have assimilated the 'Negro idiom' "; and elsewhere in the volume he even goes so far as to label a "misconception" the musicological finding "that jazz grew wholly out of 'African music.'"[3]

But the entire subject of white jazz musicians is at best irrelevant and at worst a red herring introduced to distract our attention. For what is of genuine significance so far as most jazz artists, white or black, are concerned is not the pseudoissue of whether some white musician can improvise competent jazz

---

* A small but illustrative case in point: Writing in the San Francisco "Datebook" section of the *San Francisco Chronicle* for October 15, 1978, Herb Wong asserted that trumpeter Woody Shaw was "by no means a stranger to the city[,] as he spent a couple of fruitful years here composing and performing." A quaint notion of "fruitful," I suggest, inasmuch as Shaw worked as a leader perhaps a dozen times at most in a period actually closer to four years, and finally departed simply because he could not support himself by performing in the Bay area. But for Wong to have given an accurate accounting of Shaw's local sojourn would have required him to discuss the failure of San Francisco's jazz nightclubs—principally, Keystone Korner—to offer the artist sufficient employment to survive. Taking this step assuredly would have estranged Wong (as it did this writer when he raised the matter in print) from the management of that club, made it difficult to obtain free admission, and so forth. Hence instead of the truth, we are fed fairy-tale fantasies about the "fruitful years . . . in the city" in order to misrepresent the reality of a period during which Woody Shaw in fact eked out an existence at a near-starvation level.

solos, nor even the question of that musician's ability to enrich himself by so doing. A thousand times more crucial are such matters as how much jazz is being recorded overall, to what extent are record companies willing to subsidize jazz as they do concert music in the European tradition, which firms are most unscrupulous in violating their contracts with and otherwise victimizing jazz artists, and so on. Given the enormous power possessed by recording companies and the other business enterprises of jazz to benefit or injure musicians, the policies of such firms are of inestimably greater importance to the jazz artists than, say, who deserves to have been invested with the crown of "King of Swing." But Leonard Feather, by his constant harping on the role of the white musician in jazz, serves to redirect our gaze from the essential to the ephemeral. In this way, he uses his influence to insure that the subject of greatest gravity—the control of black music and musicians by white-owned corporations, with all that situation entails—goes unexamined, undebated, and, therefore, unchallenged.

Where Feather's approach is to conceal the status quo behind a smoke screen of verbiage about the relative contributions of white and black musicians, the late Martin Williams's course (as I bring out more fully in the next chapter) was to offer, in the guise of "benevolence," an ingenious apology for that same status quo. Accordingly, in his book *The Jazz Tradition* he argued that "it does no damage to my sense of good will toward men or my belief in the equality of men, I trust, to conclude that Negroes as a race have a rhythmic genius that is not like that of other races, and to concede that this genius has found a unique expression in the United States."[4]

Seemingly a gracious acknowledgment, Willams's "concession" in reality operates only to confirm the subservient status of the black artist in jazz. For his "conclusion" that black people have a singular "rhythmic genius that is not like that of other races" is based on one, and only one, extremely weak bit of supposed "evidence": the demonstrated excellence of black musicians as jazz innovators. But now let us take this same line of reasoning—to use the term loosely—and apply it to business in general and the business institutions of jazz in particular. Utilizing Williams's own methodology, we emerge with an unavoidable result: the unquestionable skills of whites in dominating the business aspects of jazz must be the consequence of their financial "genius that is not like that of other races." Therefore, black musical malcontents should at once cease their grousing about injustice and get back to their singin', dancin', an' hollerin', pickin' dat cotton while Marse Jim and Missy Ann enjoy theyselfs sipping juleps up at de Big House. For has not Martin Williams put his personal stamp of approval on this Best of All Possible Worlds? Black people have their "rhythmic genius that is not like that of other races," allowing them to create all that wonderful music. Whites have their financial "genius that is not like that of other races," allowing *them* to reap the no-less-marvelous profits from that music. So what that for more than two and one-half centuries just such an ideology of heritable "racial" differences was invoked in defense of human slavery? After all, Martin Williams has offered us reassurances about his "sense of good will" and his "belief in the equality of men." Why be concerned about results when we can so easily comfort ourselves with noble intentions instead?

For a final example, there are the abortive passages in Nat Hentoff's book, *Jazz Is,* that purport to describe "The Political Economy of Jazz."[5] As I noted above in chapter 1, this cursory disquisition opens with a trenchant quotation from trumpeter Rex Stewart—"Where the control is, the money is"[6]—but immediately thereafter retreats to such infinitely less controversial topics as the role of jazz in school curricula, and the like. Hentoff's unseemly haste to have done with the subject means that he does not give the reader so much as a single bit of essential information about the distribution of money-cum-power within jazz, though the author's adroitness does allow him to drop a very hot potato before his hands are singed irremediably. As for gaining an understanding of the actual operations of the political economy of jazz—that, one surmises, can await a later date. *Much* later, should Mr. Hentoff have his way.

If these illustrations convey an image of intellectual dishonesty among the more prominent white "authorities" on jazz, the impression is not without foundation.

One very revealing indication of this intellectual dishonesty, as it happens, can be discerned in the reaction of white writers to my own work on black music. It may appear that this is an extraordinarily arrogant or egomaniacal statement on my part. Rest assured, it is not. In claiming that his response to my work is one index of a writer's intellectual integrity, I am not making any particular judgment regarding *the merits* (or lack of them) of anything published under my name. What I am maintaining, however, is that a *central theme* running through that work is an exploration of the principal contradiction in jazz—that between music created by black artists on the one hand and controlled by white businessmen on the other.

In the course of this exploration, moreover, I have consistently sought to uphold the side of the black artist when, as all too frequently the case, it comes into conflict with that of the white owners, managers, publishers, and journalists. And in so doing, I have not hesitated to single out, by name, those white writers most heavily involved in the manufacture and dissemination of reactionary ideology on behalf of the executives who direct the political economy of jazz.

Thus, without wishing to be tedious, it is surely pertinent in this connection that in the first edition of *Black Nationalism and the Revolution in Music*, I attempted to counter the vilification heaped upon the head of John Coltrane (and, to some extent, Eric Dolphy as well) by Leonard Feather, Ira Gitler, and Martin Williams during the early years of the 1960s, when Coltrane's music was being condemned as "anti-jazz." Again, in opposition to the efforts of the staff of *down beat* magazine to launch a Holy Crusade against the advocates of black nationalism in jazz, I wrote to defend that ideology as a comprehensible and legitimate response of black artists to the oppression of themselves and their people. In addition, I endeavored to call attention to the cynical exploitation of jazz overseas as a "Cold War secret weapon" at the same time that its black practitioners here were still being relegated to the status of third-class citizens both as artists and as individuals.[7]

I mention these things now not to compile a list of my accomplishments, but to indicate some of the reasons why I maintain that the degree of a writer's truthfulness and objectivity in dealing with the political economy of jazz can be gauged at least in part by his treatment of the body of published material associated with my name. For in handling that material in a less-than-honest fashion, a writer goes beyond simply discriminating against an opponent in a debate and instead involves himself in an attempt at suppressing altogether discussion of many of the most crucial social questions in jazz. And that, of course, is of considerably greater seriousness than the matter of how one writer chooses to react to the views of another.

At this juncture, then, it will prove enlightening if we examine the way in which my ideas have been received by four black authors and by four prominent white ones.

The very existence of a sizable number of black authors who write on jazz-related subjects is still a relatively recent phenomenon. As late as 1960, there were in print few if any major studies of jazz by black authors. Even since that time, moreover, I can call to mind the names of only about a dozen or so black authors who have written about jazz with any regularity. Besides being much fewer in number, black writers on jazz also differ from their white counterparts in three other significant respects: (1) most approach the music from a different perspective than whites, having experienced jazz in different situations and environments; (2) a higher proportion of black writers on jazz are academicians, hence better schooled than the representative white writer on jazz; and (3) as academicians or professionals, these black authors are more likely to be independent of the network of white-owned businesses that collectively dominate the political economy of jazz.

No doubt all of these considerations lead black writers, as we shall see, to be more willing to entertain views running against the grain of the white-defined orthodoxy in jazz. Thus, a highly regarded composer and instrumentalist, *Professor David Baker* of Indiana University, in his essay on "The Music and Poetry of Jazz," draws in detail on the introductory chapter of my own *Black Nationalism to* explain "why all of the major innovators in jazz have been black."[8] Thus, *O.C. Simpkins, M.D.*, in his volume *Coltrane: A Biography*, makes more extensive use of the interview I conducted with John Coltrane in 1966 and published in *Black Nationalism* in 1970—a historical document whose existence the white writers surveyed below have yet to acknowledge—than of any other single source. Thus, *Professor Bill Cole*, in his study *John Coltrane*, cites *Black Nationalism* repeatedly throughout and lists five other works of mine under the heading "For Further Reference."[9] And thus, finally, *saxophonist Nathan Davis*, a professor of music at the University of Pittsburgh, writes, "Among books, Frank Kofsky's work on black music and its revolutionary role during the 1960s, *Black Nationalism and the Revolution in Music*, is an outstanding contribution to jazz literature."[10]

Now compare the foregoing with the way in which four widely published white writers on jazz have approached my work.

The late *Martin Williams* directed the Jazz Program at the Smithsonian Institution in Washington, D.C. Inasmuch as it was written on that program's letterhead, the missive from his operative, J.R. Taylor, that appears as the epigraph to this chapter—a completely crude attempt at intimidating the editors of *The Journal of Jazz Studies* from publishing any further contributions of mine—can be taken to represent Williams's own point of view. That his opinions disagree with my own is a matter of no consequence; that he should approve, even implicitly, such a blatant effort at stifling the free expression of ideas is utterly reprehensible—though hardly astonishing.

Nat Hentoff we have already encountered at some length in chapter 1. Considering that much of *Black Nationalism and the*

Revolution in Music is devoted to a discussion of the music of
John Coltrane and certain aspects of its relationship to the political economy of jazz, and considering that Hentoff has seen
fit to write about both topics in his book *Jazz Is*, it seems sur-
passing strange that his bibliography in the latter makes no
mention of *Black Nationalism*. Stranger still, considering the
citation therein of LeRoi Jones's *Blue People* and *Black Music*,
A.B. Spellman's *Four Lives in the Bebop Business*, Simpkins's
Coltrane: A Biography (with the author's initials erroneously
listed as "C.D." instead of C.O.) and J.C. Thomas's sad excuse
for a biography, *Chasin' the Trane*.[11] But perhaps Hentoff just
never got around to reading *Black Nationalism*? Mutual ac-
quaintances assure me that such is not the case; and even if he
didn't *read* it, it defies credulity to suppose that he doesn't *know
of* it. As it is unthinkable that this oft-proclaimed champion of
unfettered discussion and First Amendment rights to freedom
of speech would be guilty of an attempt to suppress information, one can surmise only that Hentoff simply doesn't believe
that a book containing, among other things, the last major interview granted by John Coltrane—and conceivably the one
most frequently quoted as well—could possibly be of any interest to his readers. And here I had been laboring under the impression that it was only in the novels of George Orwell that living human beings were relegated to the status of "unpersons"!

For unvarnished intellectual dishonesty in practice, however,
Ira Gitler and *Leonard Feather*, the co-compilers of the *Encyclopedia of Jazz in the Seventies*, provide us with what is easily
the most flagrant example. On page 391 of this tome begins a
section entitled "Bibliography: Books 1966–1975." Included under this heading on the following page is this following entry:

RIVELLI, PAULINE & ROBERT LEVIN, Eds.,
Rock Giants, Jazz & Pop (World Publ. Co.) 125 pp. 1970.[12]

If it strikes the reader as curious that a book on rock is listed
in a bibliography of jazz works, how much more curious is it

that *Black Giants*—the companion volume on jazz musicians published *on the same day, in the same city and by the same publisher*[13]—is omitted entirely? How can it be that in the bibliography of what purports to be a jazz encyclopedia the editors cite a book of essays on rock performers while wholly ignoring the book on jazz artists intended to accompany it?

The mystery can be very simply resolved by a glance at the table of contents of *Black Giants*. The first four chapters and chapter 10 as well are all by this author; together, they comprise just under forty percent (50 pages out of 126) of the total. What is more, chapters 2 and 3 contain critical remarks in abundance by both John Coltrane and myself about the closed-minded positions taken by Feather, Gitler and Martin Williams during the "anti-jazz" polemical battles of the early 1960s— shameful historical roles these presumably chagrined writers later sought to bury as deeply and thoroughly as possible. Thus, Feather and Gitler find acceptable *Rock Giants*, which does not even treat jazz-related subjects, but by the perverse standards that govern the composition of their "Bibliography," *Black Giants* remains absolutely beyond the pale. As for *Black Nationalism and the Revolution in Music*, the question is not even worth posing: once again, an "unbook" written by an "unperson."*

If you are astounded and dismayed at the concept of "scholarship" that allows the inclusion of a title on rock but excludes two books on jazz from the bibliography of what purports to be

---

* At least, though, I have the consolation of being in good company. Under the heading "Selections for Further Reading" in the pamphlet that Martin Williams co-wrote with Ira Gitler to accompany *The Smithsonian Collection of Classic Jazz*, not only is there no mention of *Black Nationalism and the Revolution in Music*, but—a far less excusable omission—both of the books on the subject by LeRoi Jones (Amiri Baraka), *Blues People* and *Black Music*, are conspicuous by their absence. (The Williams-Gitler "Selections" do, however, contain the titles of no fewer than five volumes by the former and two by the latter.) Heaven forbid that the mind of an innocent jazz lover be contaminated by heresies from the likes of Jones or myself! Once again, it appears, when our esteemed white jazz critics set out to do battle, it is a safe bet that intellectual integrity will be among the earliest casualties.

an *encyclopedia of jazz,* you are not alone. Disputes among writers are ubiquitous and their occurrence requires no elaborate explanation. But for one author or set of authors to pretend that certain contrary views simply have not been published and do not exist—such inexcusable ethical bankruptcy is wholly beyond my comprehension.

I trust it does make clear, however, my reasons for entitling this chapter as I have.

A word about what follows. Chapter 6 is a painstaking scrutiny of one representative example of how the history of jazz should not be written, *The Jazz Tradition* by Martin Williams. Because it is not sufficient merely to criticize the way in which most white authors have tended to treat the history of jazz, however, I also have felt obliged to offer a different approach based on my own research. Accordingly, in chapter 7 I propose an alternative method for understanding the history of innovation in jazz, one rooted in the folk history of black people themselves. Whatever may be its other defects, at least it is not a rationalization of the existing distribution of revenues and rewards, in which black artists labor long and hard to create jazz music for the benefit of white owners.

NOTES

1. *The Journal of Jazz Studies,* IV:2 (Spring/Summer 1977), p. 102.

2. See in this connection "Critiquing the Critics," chapter 3 in Frank Kofsky, *John Coltrane and the Jazz Revolution of the 1960s* (New York: Pathfinder Press, 1998), the second, revised and expanded edition of *Black Nationalism and the Revolution in Music.*

3. See Leonard Feather, *The New Edition of the Encyclopedia of Jazz* (New York: Horizon Press, 1960), pp. 22–23, 82–86; and, as a necessary corrective, Gunther Schuller's elucidation of the African origins of the salient elements of jazz, chapter 1 in *Early Jazz: Its Roots and Musical Development* (New York: Oxford University Press, 1968).

4. Martin Williams, *The Jazz Tradition,* (New York: Oxford University Press, 1970), pp. 7–8.

5. See Nat Hentoff, *Jazz Is* (New York: Avon Press, 1978), pp. 257–64.

6. Quoted in *Jazz Is*, p. 257.

7. I refer the reader to my book, *John Coltrane and the Jazz Revolution of the 1960s*, for the details.

8. See David Baker, "The Music and Poetry of Jazz," in *Humanities Through the Black Experience* (Dubuque, Iowa: Kendall-Hunt Publishing Co., 1977), Phyllis Rauch Klotman, ed., pp. 119–22; the quotation, which introduces a lengthy excerpt from *Black Nationalism*, is on p. 120. Note that Baker's position on this question is, not unexpectedly, diametrically opposed to the one espoused by Leonard Feather.

9. See O.C. Simpkins, M.D., *Coltrane: A Biography* (Brooklyn, New York: Herndon House, 1975); Bill Cole, *John Coltrane* (New York: Schirmer Books, 1976), p. 247. Lest it be thought that Simpkins and Cole were compelled to refer to *Black Nationalism* simply because both wrote books on the life of John Coltrane, it should be observed a supposed biography of the saxophonist by a white author—J.C. Thomas, *Chasin' the Trane: The Music and Mystique of John Coltrane* (New York: Doubleday, 1975)—makes no mention at all either of *Black Nationalism and the Revolution in Music* nor its author. Not, however, that this omission hinders Thomas in the least from using without attribution, as I have elsewhere remarked, material taken from *Black Nationalism*; see my review essay "Missin' the Trane: Three Flawed Works on John Coltrane," *The Journal of Ethnic Studies*, VI:1 (Spring 1978), p. 89.

10. Nathan T. Davis, *Writings in Jazz*, 5th ed. (Dubuque, Iowa: Kendall-Hunt Publishing, 1996), p. 205.

11. See Hentoff, *Jazz Is*, p. 286.

12. Leonard Feather and Ira Gitler, comps., *The Encyclopedia of Jazz in the Seventies* (New York: Horizon Press, 1976), pp. 391–92.

13. Pauline Rivelli and Robert Levin, eds., *Black Giants* (Jazz & Pop and World Publishing Co.: New York, 1970).

Charlie Parker

BESSIE
SMITH

Exclusive Columbia
Phonograph Artist

Bessie Smith

Billie Holiday

VAL WILMER

Thelonious Monk

VAL WILMER

Dexter Gordon

VAL WILMER

Jackie McClean

Ornette Coleman Quartet (1971)

VAL WILMER

Miles Davis

6

The 'jazz tradition':
black music, white critic

For the reader who wishes a superficial work on jazz written from an avowedly anti-Marxist perspective by an author who confesses that he is "repeatedly disengaged" by the post-1960 music of John Coltrane, Martin Williams's *The Jazz Tradition*[1] should fit the bill perfectly.*

Were it simply a matter of Williams's book alone, the matter could be left at that. Implicitly at stake, however, is an issue of much larger and more significant dimensions: who is to have custody over the interpretation of black music, and what uses will its future custodians make of it? Leaving aside the particular merits, or lack of them, of Williams's work, this is a question of sufficient importance to demand our attention.

To my knowledge, the question was first raised in recent

---

* Williams expands his complaint about Coltrane: "After three or four minutes my attention wanders, and giving the records try after try does not seem to help." Further comment on my part would be superfluous. See *The Jazz Tradition*, p. 202.

times by LeRoi Jones in his 1963 essay on "Jazz and the White Critic" (subsequently reprinted in his 1968 anthology *Black Music*). There, Jones noted that historically the music has been almost entirely created by blacks but almost entirely interpreted by whites, and that—given the immense cultural and intellectual chasm that separates the "races" in the United States—the consequences of this situation have been almost unrelievedly disastrous for those seeking to comprehend the essence of this black music.[2] Thereafter, in an essay of my own in the first edition of *Black Nationalism and the Revolution in Music*, I tried to amplify some of Jones's insights and show specific examples of the way in which white critics were even then making efforts to suppress the epochal innovations of John Coltrane, Ornette Coleman, Cecil Taylor, and other artists of that eminence.[3] Though these analyses did succeed in generating a certain amount of polemical heat, basically they changed nothing. The result is that all the questions about criticism brought up in the 1960s are still in need of discussion and resolution. There is, of course, no guarantee that a second march over the same terrain will produce a different outcome than the first. Nonetheless, the entire social and intellectual climate is vastly different from what it was then, and for that reason these remarks may fall on more fertile ground than their predecessors.

To the lay listener, any discourse on criticism (as opposed to a discourse about the music itself) may seem an unnecessary imposition. After all, he or she may be thinking, my interest is not in reading what critics have to say about each other, but in learning something that will enhance my appreciation of the music. And well it should be! The only problem is that it falls to the critic—who ideally ought to serve as a connecting link between performer and public—to provide the listener with the maximum possible illumination. As long as this is the case, there is no point pretending that discussions about criticism are somehow irrelevant; that is merely evading the issue. In the long run, some would argue, a truly significant artist will come to enjoy great esteem, regardless of what critics may once have written.

Ah, but the long run may be very long indeed. Critics are still arguing the relative merits of Jelly Roll Morton's music. Jelly Roll himself, however, had the bad grace to expire before the debate had concluded, at a time when his work was still obscure to many lovers of jazz. Few artists would care to recapitulate that experience; most, understandably enough, prefer somewhat speedier recognition. And with this we are once more back to the critics.

Like it or not, it is the critics who, in the short run, often serve as the arbiters of taste and tradition, defining what is "good" and what is "bad" in jazz—sometimes to the point where musicians out of critical favor find it difficult (or worse) to obtain work. This is no idle flight of fancy, as Thelonious Monk, to name but one, readily could have testified after a decade of marginal existence between the late 1940s and the late 1950s. Inasmuch as the critics, taken collectively, can wield power to that degree, it is a matter of no small importance—to the listener as well as the performer—to inquire more closely: Who are the critics? And how do they do what it is they do?

If one looks retrospectively at jazz criticism in this country since the music's inception, it takes little time to perceive that the most lasting works have ordinarily fallen in one of two categories: (1) musicological analysis; (2) social interpretation. Classic examples of the former are André Hodeir's justly celebrated book *Jazz: Its Evolution and Essence*, and, more recently, Gunther Schuller's study *Early Jazz*.[4] What distinguishes a Hodeir or a Schuller from his fellow critics is not merely the ability to transcribe a solo as it is played on record. Leonard Feather is a critic with sufficient musical training to do the latter; but none of his works, to my way of thinking, displays anything like the insightful qualities of the volumes of Hodeir and Schuller.*
Beyond mere technical accomplishment, the skilled musicolo-

---

* As my disagreements with Feather, on both social and artistic questions, are by now sufficiently numerous and widely broadcast to be legendary, it is mandatory that I make myself as clear as possible. I am in no sense denigrating Feather's ability as a musicologist, nor disputing his contribution as a compiler of encyclopedias. What I am saying, conversely, is that there is nothing of his

gist must bring to jazz a warm enthusiasm for his subject, the taste (that perhaps cannot be formally taught) to know which artists and which works will repay the employment of his or her skills, and an intuitive, empathetic rapport that allows the analyst to recapture the thinking that has gone into the creation of a given composition or solo. All of this, needless to say, requires considerably more than the relatively straightforward capacity to transcribe a piece of music from a phonograph recording.

The second type of work on jazz that has demonstrated its durability over the long haul has been the social analysis that treats jazz (and other forms of black music) as a manifestation of the Afro-American experience. Examples of this genre in English that spring readily to mind are LeRoi Jones's *Blues People* (and portions of *Black Music*), A.B. Spellman's *Four Lives in the Bebop Business*, Sidney Finkelstein's *Jazz: A People's Music*, and Francis Newton's (that is, E.J. Hobsbawm's) *The Jazz Scene.*[5] What all of these books have in common, either formally or informally, consciously or unconsciously, is their dependence on Marxian ideas for a frame of reference (in the case of Hobsbawm and Finkelstein, the Marxist mode of analysis is fairly

that has enriched my understanding of the music of an artist as Hodeir has in the case of Parker or Schuller has in the case of Morton. This, moreover, has nothing whatsoever to do with the social views of either of these two authors. Both of them, for example, appear to believe, as does Martin Williams (*Jazz Tradition*, pp. 7–8), that the musical gifts of Afro-Americans and Africans are transmitted genetically (by nature) rather than socially (by nurture). Feather disputes this point (see, for example, Chapter 5 of *The Book of Jazz* [New York: Meridian Books, 1959]), and on this issue I side with him. Regardless of their views in this regard, however, the analyses by Hodeir and Schuller are far and away outstanding examples of their kind. A comparison of their writing with that of Feather should also establish beyond question that technical knowledge of music, in and of itself, offers no guarantee that its possessor will employ it with skill and discretion. It is notorious, to take one case in point, that all of Feather's knowledge of music did not prevent him from condemning the work of John Coltrane as "anti-jazz" early in the 1960s (see Frank Kofsky, *John Coltrane and the Jazz Revolution of the 1960s* [New York: Pathfinder Press, 1998], chapter 8, for the grim details). Musical expertise, like any other, can either be used or misused, depending on the possessor.

explicit). However reprehensible this may seem to Williams and those critics who endorse his views, this use of Marxist analysis is not only not surprising but is, in fact, quite predictable. Inasmuch as Marxism holds that a people's literature, art, philosophy, and so on, arise out of and generally reflect the material conditions of that group's social existence, it follows that anyone who interprets jazz or black music in terms of the history of African-Americans must necessarily have recourse to concepts and ideas that, in the broadest sense, derive from Marxism. It ought to go without saying (but probably doesn't) that the mere use of Marxian ideas as an analytical tool in no way guarantees that any given individual will be a sensitive and acute commentator on the music, any more than being able to read and write music insures that a critic always displays sound judgment, discretion, and an open mind. Just as with musicology, Marxism has not lacked its share of hacks and dogmatists. There simply are no short cuts to, much less substitutes for, critical judiciousness, empathy, lucidity, and the flexibility and openness to absorb the lessons of the best teachers of all, the jazz musicians themselves.*

The majority of books dealing with jazz, especially those written by white American authors, have not withstood the test of time nearly so well as the ones I noted above. To comprehend the reasons for this at once forces us to confront the historical (and contemporary) dilemma of white jazz criticism, a dilemma that both LeRoi Jones and myself (and probably others as well) have tried to bring to the attention of the jazz public. Typically, the white author of books about jazz has been neither a trained

---

* Both in *Blues People* and *Black Music*, LeRoi Jones remarks that to be black automatically makes one a nonconformist in the United States. Apparently, the same rule applies even to those who would understand on its own terms the black music produced in this country. Consider: Jones and A.B. Spellman are African-Americans; Hodeir is French; Hobsbawm-Newton is British and a Marxist to boot; and Finkelstein is also a Marxist. It is almost as if to say that before one can grasp the essence of black music, one must in one way or another step outside the standard viewpoint and attitudes of the middle-class white "mainstream."

musicologist nor a committed Marxist scholar. More often than not, he has brought little to his writing except quantities of enthusiasm for his favorite artists, plus a few vague efforts at aesthetic pronouncements and musical descriptions, both of which usually have lacked precision and been unrelated to any body of theory about anything. Such authors undoubtedly mean well—but good intentions have never yet been worth much when all the other ingredients for success are lacking. Unable to formulate and illustrate his artistic judgments in precise musical terms, devoid of a social theory that might tighten and unify his work, our hapless writer is doomed to end up with a polyglot pastiche that never jells—here a chronology, there a stab at relating jazz to the lives of black people, somewhere else a compilation of apocrypha about the glorious days and deeds in Chicago, New York, the Mississippi. In short, a muddle—one that adds little to our comprehension of the music and one whose main raison d'être is its author's eagerness to leave posterity a record of the devotion he feels toward "his" music. Barry Ulanov's *A History of Jazz in America* is a better-than-average representative of this scattergun approach for the 1950s; its latter-day equivalent, I suspect, will not look too much different from *The Jazz Tradition* by Martin Williams (or, to refer back to Chapter 1, *Jazz Is* by Nat Hentoff).[6]

One might maintain that, aside from the fact that works of this nature do not sell very many copies and thus help to convince publishers that there is no market for that rarity, a truly valuable book on jazz, these volumes are for the most part harmless. Perhaps ten or twenty years ago, such a proposition was defensible. Today, however, matters stand somewhat differently. On the one hand, there is an intense thirst on the part of black youth to learn about their past. On the other, there is anything but a demand for more white "experts" to confuse the historical record still further. It is not inconceivable that a time may come when it will be impossible for a white author to address himself to an audience on any topic that relates even remotely to the lives of black people. Should such a situation come to pass, white jazz critics, despite some distinguished exceptions to the general rule, will have done more than their share toward bringing it about.

With that in mind, I would like to scrutinize Williams's book in detail—not because it is so much better or worse than the average, but precisely because it is so representative of what white jazz criticism has amounted to historically. It may be naive, but one yet may hope that by illustrating in depth Williams's shortcomings, his successors may be able to sidestep at least some of the pitfalls that lie in wait to trap the unwary.

After completing *The Jazz Tradition*, my initial response was to wonder why on earth it ever had been written (or for that matter, published). A book that defined, illuminated, and analyzed the evolution of "the jazz tradition" would indeed be welcome, but Williams makes no real attempt at that. His introductory chapter, where one would expect an author to advance some sort of general theoretical framework, is instead (as we shall see) a compendium of offhand remarks, the substance of which is Williams's double-barreled assertion of his anti-Marxist position and his corollary conclusion "that Negroes *as a race* [my italics] have a rhythmic genius that is not like that of other races, and . . . that this genius has found a unique expression in the United States."[7] The remaining chapters are merely a series of brief sketches, which, taken collectively, fail to offer sufficient new insights and discoveries to justify the volume, still less its ambitious title. For the 1920s, Gunther Schuller's study, *Early Jazz* is infinitely more rewarding than Williams's treatment of Armstrong, Morton, and early Ellington; Williams on Charlie Parker is positively clumsy in comparison to the essay by Hodeir in *Jazz: Its Evolution and Its Essence;* and the new music can be studied to much better advantage in the works of Jones (especially *Black Music*), Spellman's book, *Four Lives*, or even the first edition of my own volume, *Black Nationalism*. In summary, therefore, *The Jazz Tradition* is a work that adds virtually nothing to our store of knowledge and, aside from the few royalties it may have earned its author, is about as superfluous a volume as can be imagined.

Let no one think, however, that Williams's inability to produce a major work on jazz is in any way due to the fact that all the critical and aesthetic problems revolving around the music have been asked and answered. Nothing could be further from the truth. Williams himself, in fact, does manage to stumble inadvertently over some important issues, but his mindless opposition to a Marxian interpretation is so all-encompassing that he can barely perceive a significant question even after stubbing his toe on it. His chances of blundering onto the answer in this fashion are about the same as those of a blindfolded dart-thrower hitting the target from across the room.

Williams's assumption that black people have "natural rhythm" is the logical by-product of his opposition to Marxian interpretations; together, these two related attitudes provide him with a set of blinkers so rigid that it would be a miracle of sorts if he were able to look beyond them long enough to formulate any conclusions worthy of consideration.* They demand to be dealt with together, simply because once one has rejected a social interpretation of black music, one must have a different interpretation to be put in its place. In itself, I suppose this could be construed as some meager sign of "progress": at least by 1970, white authors were at last finding it difficult to write a book about black music while continuing to deny that it *is*, after all, black music.

But if it is that, what makes it so? The Marxist critics have answered that all forms of black music are, *among other things*, a response to the endless oppression of black people in this country, and that the development of the various strains of the music are best understood in light of the changing circumstances

---

* As witness his ludicrous comment to author and scholar Krin Gabbard, who had had the audacity to assert that even writing about the music of an oppressed group like black Americans was a political act: "That is a basic Marxist-Leninist idea, as you may be aware. . . . I do say explicitly . . . that I reject Marxism." Martin Williams to Krin Gabbard, June 12, 1991; a copy of this letter is in the author's possession.

of those people. Having denied the validity of this approach and no longer able to skirt the issue of the Afro-American genesis of all major styles in jazz, Williams in effect backs himself into a corner with only one way out. If jazz does not represent the social creation of black people, then it can only represent—what else?—their "natural rhythm." There is no third alternative, no middle path. Having excluded the possibility of a social interpretation, he has no other choice but to account for every aspect of black music in terms of hereditary "rhythmic genius." Williams's insistence on the irrelevance of a social interpretation is thus complemented by his assumption of innate racial differences.

The baleful effects of these two postulates on Williams's book can hardly be exaggerated. To begin with, by assuming innate racial differences, Williams, *regardless of his subjective intentions,* lends his implicit support to the existing division of labor, income, and profits within the jazz world, an arrangement succinctly described by Archie Shepp: "You *own* the music and we *make* it" (my italics). Williams argues that it "does no damage to my sense of good will toward men or my belief in the equality of men" to assert that "Negroes *as a race* [sic] have a rhythmic genius that is not like that of other races."[8] He could not be more mistaken. To begin with, anthropologists have demonstrated that the concept of "race" is not a scientifically valid one, so that the very idea of "Negroes as a race" is little more than high-sounding nonsense. Particularly so in a country such as the United States, whose Afro-American population is an ethnic mixture drawn from various parts of Africa and even further removed from a mythical state of "racial purity" by combinations with various European, Asian, and American Indian strains. (The usual estimate is that upwards of 80 percent of the "blacks" in the United States have at least one ancestor of European stock.) In light of all this, what meaning can possibly attach to the notion of "Negroes as a race"?

Yet even if this notion were scientifically defensible, it would still do precisely what Williams claims it does not do—that is, put him on the side of those who deny "the equality of men."

For if we posit that black people "have a rhythmic genius" on the grounds that they have provided the dominant impulses in American popular music and culture generally, what is to stop us from concluding with equal facility that white people "have a financial genius" that makes it "only natural" that they control the recording companies, booking agencies, jazz nightclubs and festivals, and so on, to the exclusion of almost all blacks? Clearly, whites must have this innate talent—just look at how many great businessmen they have produced! And likewise for the field of jazz criticism, which, overall, has been a vehicle for white rather than black writers.

How convenient it is that this arrangement, which patently benefits whites at the expense of blacks, can now be defended by white ideologues on the basis of inherent racial traits. Williams may deny that this was his purpose. Be that as it may, in contending that Afro-American music is to be explained on the basis of racial characteristics, he has opened a Pandora's box containing all manner of racist arguments, not least those designed to buttress the status quo. I am prepared to believe that such may not have been his intentions, but I do not see how that can render his assumptions any more palatable once one sees their unavoidable outcome. Though he may shrink from following his ideas to their inevitable conclusion, in point of fact the argument that whites, by virtue of their inherent "financial genius," belong in control of the business aspects of jazz is neither more nor less legitimate intellectually than Williams's thesis that "Negroes as a race have a rhythmic genius." The evidence for the former is of the same type as, and is exactly as good as, the evidence for the latter—which is to say that there is no evidence at all.*

---

* Any assertion about any group of abilities being innate in any population is, at this state of human knowledge, a blind leap of faith and nothing else. The truth of the matter is that as yet science has no conclusive evidence about the transmission of such abilities by inheritance in large populations. What is the case is that one cannot have one's cake and eat it too. If Williams wishes to postulate the "natural" rhythmic gifts of blacks, then he is in no position to object on theo-

If the social consequences of Williams's assumption of an innate black rhythmic sense are pernicious, the aesthetic consequences are no less so. For in postulating that jazz is an expression of this innate ability, Williams necessarily precludes his being able to ask any meaningful questions about the causes and timing of *changes* in jazz styles. The critic who utilizes a social interpretation will strive to make sense of these changes by correlating them with contemporaneous developments in the black community and the larger society. Williams, in rejecting Marxism for genetic determinism, has denied himself that option. Yes, changes certainly have taken place: musicians at one time played in the style of Louis Armstrong, whereas later they tended more to follow Charlie Parker. But as for what forces brought about these and other stylistic shifts, what causes were at the root of sudden, dramatic twists and turns in the history of jazz—to these and all related questions, Williams, as he must, remains mute. His "answer" is a shrug of the shoulders.

In no sense, therefore, can Martin Williams's book be said to merit the title *The Jazz Tradition*. By excluding social interpretations at the outset, Williams not only renders himself inca-

---

retical grounds when racists argue for the no less "natural" intellectual superiority of whites, and then bring forward endless mountains of spurious "evidence" to demonstrate, say, the evils of sending white children to school with blacks. (There are evils involved, but as Mary Ellen Goodman showed in her study, *Race Awareness in Young Children* [New York: Macmillan, 1964], they are generally perpetrated not on whites but on blacks, who are subtly taught by white peers and teachers that in practice, black means inferior.) To be sure, one cannot prove that blacks do not have such "natural" rhythm, any more than Williams can prove that whites who score higher on culturally biased IQ tests do not have "natural" intellectual superiority. But proving the nonexistence of a thing through logic alone is notoriously an impossible task. I cannot prove, for example, that there is not an invisible genie in the middle drawer on the right-hand side of my desk. But by the same token, my inability to prove the genie's absence does not mean that I am obliged to assert that he is present. The point is, if it cannot be shown that a certain thing does not exist, neither is that sufficient cause for proclaiming that it does. Lacking conclusive evidence either way, the question is necessarily moot. So while fools may rush in where angels, with good reason, fear to tread, more prudent souls will prefer to think twice before placing their feet upon such treacherous ground.

pable of explaining what that tradition is, but he also guarantees that he will be unable to discover the reasons why it is what it is and not otherwise. To comprehend the jazz tradition requires more than acquiring a smattering of information about Armstrong, Morton, Ellington, Parker, Monk, and Coltrane. It requires being able to locate each artist accurately in the context of his time, grasping the way in which his music crystallized out of that specific historical matrix, understanding how that music both built on and simultaneously rejected the legacy of jazz's past, and finally, perceiving why, at a certain point, the innovations of one group of artists were forced to make way for those of their successors. All of these problems must be addressed, if not always resolved, in terms of concrete historical circumstances; only then will a work live up to the claim of having illuminated at least the major contours of the jazz tradition. There is no more dramatic testimony to the bankruptcy of Williams's methodology than his quite apparent failure to recognize that such crucial questions must be posed in any genuine investigation of the jazz tradition.

It may be useful at this point to introduce some illustrations of how Williams's specific shortcomings flow directly out of his theoretical inadequacies. Consider first, then, the question of why bebop had to wait until the 1940s for its birth. To state the question in this fashion ought to help us apprehend the music more fully, for in the course of answering it, we will have to determine, if possible, why the innovations of bop met acceptance among musicians precisely when they did and not, for instance, a decade earlier or later. That is to say, for black musicians of the 1940s, bebop evidently was an answer to some new felt need that had not been present in previous years. By understanding what that need was, we put ourselves in a better position to respond to the qualities in bebop that enabled it to sweep through the fraternity of black musicians, the younger ones especially, like wildfire; and thereby we gain new insight into the tangible meaning of the jazz tradition at a decisive moment in its development.

We might begin by noting that, according to evidence supplied by Williams himself, the invention of bebop in the 1930s was by no means beyond the scope of existing musical knowledge in jazz, inasmuch as the procedure for improvising a solo on a set of chords

> had become a norm and commonplace by the late thirties to men like Teddy Wilson, Henry "Red" Allen, Roy Eldridge, Johnny Hodges, Ben Webster, Lester Young, Coleman Hawkins, Charlie Christian, and hundreds of others; . . . [and for that matter] one can find choruses of non-thematic improvisation in the recordings of players who were leaders in the 'twenties and earlier. . . .
>
> The practices are, basically, as old as the blues. . . . One might say that jazz musicians spent the late 'twenties and the 'thirties discovering that they could "play the blues" on chords of [the numerous popular songs of the period].[9]

Moreover, Charlie Parker, who stood at the head of the bebop revolt against swing, did not so much invent his music from scratch as he did recast material that was already present in jazz. As a case in point, one is "brought up short by the realization that a 'typical' Parker phrase turns out to be much the same phrase one had heard years before from, say, Ben Webster."[10] All of this being so, wouldn't it be reasonable to expect that bebop might have taken shape much earlier?

Considered strictly as a *musical problem*, it does indeed seem as if bebop could have been perfected several years before its actual arrival in the 1940s. What delayed its entry was less a matter of musical development than of extra-musical considerations. Among black artists generally, the mood of the 1920s was one of a cautious but definite optimism that "that great day" of full and equal participation in American society was at most just around the next corner. Hence Alain Locke, in editing the anthology *The New Negro* (1925)—the single work that best distills the attitudes of the generally middle-class black artists of the period—could point to the "renewed and keen curiosity" about Afro-American life as "an augury of a new democracy in American culture." Similarly, in his *History of Black Manhattan* (originally published in 1930), James Weldon Johnson—who, as the field secretary of the National Association for the Advancement of Colored People, can scarcely be accused of being an Uncle Tom—claimed that "more than two-hundred thousand Negroes live in the heart of Manhattan . . . and do so without race friction. These two-hundred thousand Negroes have made themselves an integral part of New York citizenry." As "New York guarantees her Negro citizens the fundamental rights of citizenship and protects them in the exercise of those rights," Johnson expected that "the Negro in New York ought to be able to work through the discriminations and disadvantages."

Black artists and intellectuals were not naive; they were well aware that only a few years before some of the bloodiest mass violence ever witnessed in the United States had been unleashed against black people in Northern cities (East St. Louis in 1917, Chicago in 1919, were two of the most gruesome instances). The largest mass movement among blacks to that time, that led by Marcus Garvey, coalesced as a result of the wartime and postwar frustrations of black people; and even though the great bulk of the artists and intellectuals held themselves aloof from the Garvey movement, as Robert A. Bone has pointed out, they could not help but be affected by Garvey's clarion calls for black pride and unity. Nonetheless, on balance they tended to believe that the black community, speaking through its artist-intellectuals, could become what Locke called a "conscious contributor," a "collaborator and participant in American civilization." In this forward step, the role of the artist would be primary, for, according to the same author, it was "cultural recognition" that would "prove the key to the re-evaluation of the Negro which must precede or accompany any considerable further betterment in race relationships."[11]

Black art, in other words, was going to be consciously, even quasi-nationalistically, employed to promote—integration. Such ambivalence may not have been strictly logical, but it was understandably pervasive. It extended, moreover, to music as well as the other arts. It is perhaps ironic that Duke Ellington, who is today revered for his elaboration of Afro-American folk materials into a body of formal music, should have begun his career attempting to emulate the "symphonic jazz" associated with Paul Whiteman and others; but, as Gunther Schuller remarks, "there seems to have been a greater effort on the part of Northeastern Negroes to assimilate with the whites, especially in the field of music." Actually, however, such attempts were by no means restricted to music. On the contrary, they were part of the intellectual baggage of all of the 1920s "New Negroes," who, even as they turned to the heritage of their people as a source of inspiration, were careful to keep a weather eye cocked on the reception their works were receiving from their white counterparts.[12]

Far from weakening this tentative faith in an ultimately integrated future, the Great Depression of the 1930s only strengthened it. For once, large numbers of white people were abruptly thrown into something like the same situation that black people had experienced ever since shattering the chains of chattel slavery—a rough-and-ready de facto integration carried out by poverty, if you will. Coupled with this was the fact that new institutions were appearing, and some of them were open to black participation. Black intellectuals joined the Communist Party. Black workers joined the new industrial unions that comprised the Congress of Industrial Organizations (CIO). The black poor received some benefits from various New Deal agencies, even though most of these distributed their meager favors in a flagrantly discriminatory manner. Along with Italians, Poles, Jews, and various other ethnic groups, blacks swung into line behind the Roosevelt coalition. Correspondingly, nationalism's overt adherents dwindled to scattered handfuls of individuals in a few isolated sects.

Many of these attitudes were reversed, however, with the

coming of World War II. Here, one can do no better than quote
James Baldwin, whose reaction was representative:

> The treatment accorded the Negro during the Second World
> War marks, for me, a turning point in the Negro's relation to
> America. To put it briefly, and somewhat too simply, a certain
> hope died, a certain respect for white America faded.[13]

The list of causes for this radical shift in attitude is long, but
in essence can be boiled down to the fact that every aspect of
Washington's conduct of the war, from employment opportunities in war-production industries to the role of blacks in the
armed services, was pervaded by racism, at the same time that
blacks were being pushed to support a crusade allegedly directed
against the "master race" doctrines of the Axis powers.

We may now return to the question of the genesis of bebop.
As should be clear from the above, the 1940s were a period of
unrest and ferment for black people; and their indignation at
the racist methods with which the United States chose to wage
what was officially described as "a battle for democracy" necessarily *had to* spill over into the music of that era (as I demonstrate in much greater depth in chapter 1 of *John Coltrane and
the Jazz Revolution of the 1960s*). Eric Hobsbawm has correctly
noted that during this decade the "political awakening of all the
oppressed and underprivileged . . . put a new tone" into the black
musician's instrument: "open resentment."[14] In addition to their
outrage over the indignities to which all black people were being subjected, young musicians were further incensed that white
performers had been reaping the cream of the benefits from a
black invention, swing music. And, as Leslie B. Rout has written, hiring a few blacks to play in otherwise all-white bands only

> increased black discontent, because from the black musician's
> point of view, acceptance into white orchestras demonstrated
> how badly black swingsters were needed! Why, then, be satis-
> fied with a few crumbs, while "Whitey" took cake?

Why indeed? The black musician's logical next move was to give concrete substance to his grievances by creating, in Professor Rout's words,

> a jazz form that whites could not play! Ideally, this would insure for black jazzmen the recognition they craved, plus a lion's share of the profits.[15]

Hence bebop was more than just a set of musical procedures; it was also a musical vehicle for expressing black dissatisfaction with the status quo. Nor is this consideration at all extraneous to the music itself, for we can understand bebop's hard emotional edge only in this context. The mere fact that many of these same bebop pioneers—drummers Kenny Clarke and Art Blakey, saxophonist Shahib Shahab, trumpeter Kenny Dorham, pianist Walter Bishop, Jr.—turned their back on Christianity ("the white man's religion") to embrace Islam surely has relevance to the music they played with such great intensity.[16]

Inasmuch as, according to Martin Williams himself, all the strictly musical techniques and devices that formed the foundation for bebop were already well known prior to the musical revolution of the 1940s, we can assert with some confidence that the decisive additional ingredient that detonated the revolution was the anger with which young blacks greeted the nation's failure to implement the democratic ideology employed as a psychological weapon in World War II. So much would seem to be a commonplace, had not white jazz critics gone out of their way in an attempt to dissociate the music from the social forces that helped to shape it. In this context, we should, as I suggested in the previous chapter, view Williams's aversion to a social interpretation as an affirmation of white critical orthodoxy rather than as an individual idiosyncrasy. Thus Ira Gitler, another white critic who lays claim to some expertise on the music (if not the history) of this period, dogmatically refuses to concede any social significance to bebop. Pressed for the meaning of the title of saxophonist Charlie Parker's blues composition, "Now's the Time," Gitler's reply is most instructive:

> I deny any "obvious social implication." The title refers to the music and the "now" was the time for the people to dig it.[17]

We can best evaluate Gitler's thesis by looking at the life of the musician who, more than any other, symbolized the bebop revolution. It is plain on the face of it that Charlie Parker did not blink at the risk of death as the price of expressing his deep-seated antipathy to racism.

Two illustrations suffice. On one Arkansas night in 1943, an unarmed Parker faced down and forced into retreat a white thug who, wielding a beer bottle, had just put a gash that required stitches in the head of Dizzy Gillespie.[18] The following year, the saxophonist was working in St. Louis in the big band of singer Billy Eckstine; the group was playing at a so-called black-and-tan cabaret that employed only black performers, but served only white patrons. When the management refused to let the musicians enter the front door or associate with the clientele, Parker's response exemplified his brilliant, unorthodox cast of mind. While the other musicians were relaxing during an intermission, Parker went to them one by one and asked for the glass from which each had been drinking, and at the end of his rounds broke all of the glasses at once. The "explanation" he offered to the incredulous proprietor was that he was sure the cabaret would not wish to serve its regular customers from a vessel "contaminated" (Parker's word, quoted by drummer Art Blakey) by the lips of a black person. The owner, a notorious St. Louis gangster (a combination of professions, alas, all too common in jazz), arrived in the midst of this amazing performance and was only narrowly dissuaded from doing violence to the musician. But Parker was so incensed at racist assaults on his human dignity that he was oblivious to the danger he courted in venting the hostility and resentment these insults inspired.[19]

Because of the systematic pattern of distortion that white

critics have imposed on the history of jazz, it is now necessary to try with equal thoroughness to uncover its past. Only in this way will we ever be able to rediscover for ourselves something of the meaning that the music had for its creators and for those who were present to witness its birth. For this reason we must insist at every step of the way that jazz (and black music generally) cannot be wrenched from its social moorings if there is ever to be an intelligent discussion of "the jazz tradition." The point is a crucial one. Whatever may comprise the jazz tradition, certainly we can expect it to emerge at its clearest by a careful study of those periods in which the music is changing most drastically and rapidly. For it is primarily in such periods—when a multitude of directions are possible, but only one is chosen—that the tradition most explicitly defines itself. The bebop revolution, like the earlier stylistic shifts associated with Morton, Armstrong, and Ellington, presents the jazz tradition to us, as it were, in the process of becoming. If, therefore, we can unravel the complex skein of specific forces that propelled the bebop revolution along certain paths rather than others (in the direction of Charlie Parker instead of, say, Stan Kenton), we will have a much greater appreciation of what it means to speak of "the jazz tradition."

It is exactly problems of this nature that Williams's methodology is incapable of solving. Ironically, although Williams claims to believe in an inherent black rhythmic sense, from the way in which he writes about Charlie Parker and bebop, Parker could as well have been a Martian as an Afro-American. In practice, it turns out that Williams's assumption of innate rhythmic abilities is wholly gratuitous, simply because there is no way in which he can apply this postulate to such concrete historical questions as why the bebop revolution took place only in the 1940s or how this revolution served to redefine the jazz tradition. As his intellectual frame of reference is totally inadequate for dealing with such theoretical issues, Williams is compelled to bypass them as if they did not exist, in the process once again giving the lie to his choice of title. The primary task of anyone seeking to illuminate the jazz tradition is to show as precisely as possible how this tradition came into being over a period of several decades. Williams's failure to confront this question in his account of something so fundamental as the bebop revolution is a glaring demonstration of the unproductive character of his key assumptions.

A second and related failure occurs near the end of Williams's chapter on Charlie Parker, in a discussion of the fact that the bebop artists "proposed a change in the function of the music." After noting that bebop was not a music meant for dancing—a point disputed by LeRoi Jones, incidentally[20]—Williams goes on to remark that "for a large segment of its audience" bebop is nonetheless

> not quite an art music or a concert music. It remains by and large still something of a barroom atmosphere music. And perhaps a failure to establish a new function and milieu for jazz was, more than anything else, the personal tragedy of the members of the bebop generation.[21]

Were Williams not so narrowly anti-Marxist in his approach, he might have been aware that, more than two decades earlier, Sidney Finkelstein had wrestled at length with just this problem in his book, *Jazz: A People's Music.* Here again, Williams's choice of assumptions sabotages his criticism. The attempt by Parker and his contemporaries to liberate jazz from its utterly unsuitable saloon surroundings, as well as those vagaries of Parker's personality that Williams refers to so insensitively,[22] sprang from the situation of the black musician in the 1940s. It does not require great insight to realize that Parker and his peers regarded what they did as art, and that, both as artists and sensitive black men, they were determined to demand for their work the same respect that so-called serious white composers and performers obtained as a matter of course.

All of this was grasped as long ago as 1948 by Finkelstein, who had the good sense not to accuse the bebop revolutionaries of "a failure to establish a new function and milieu for jazz," but instead advanced a series of proposals that, if implemented, would have revitalized all aspects of American music, jazz not least among them. Finkelstein called for a broad program of public support for jazz in the form of local community-sponsored jazz bands, the integration of jazz and folk musics with regional theater groups, the incorporation of courses in the playing and composition of jazz in the "music schools, conservatories and music departments of the universities," and so on. Not only would these steps have served to "remove much of the unwholesome atmosphere that now afflicts jazz—the exhausting travel, the one-night stands, the nightclub madness, the financial insecurity, the long hours, the unsettled home life," but they also might have injected a little welcome vigor into American art music, then as now an often lifeless, second-rate body of works manifesting all too clearly the unhealthy effects of being long divorced from their popular and folk roots.[23]

Why, then, did such developments not occur? The answer is anything but obscure. As Finkelstein himself appreciated, "Fundamental to all of these plans is the abolition of all forms of discrimination against minority peoples, as devastating to our music and cultural life as it is to our economic life and democracy."[24] Given the fact that no such attack on racism ever took place, the outcome was predictable. Just as black people were only rarely allowed to benefit from the material fruits of the society their labors had built, so were black artists rigidly confined to the most ill-paying, cramped, and anti-artistic circumstances. For the jazz musician, this meant that the nightclub would continue to be one of the main sources of sustenance, regardless of how inhospitable that environment might be for a sophisticated music such as bebop.

Though this state of affairs was indeed, in Williams's words, "the personal tragedy of the members of the bebop generation," one can scarcely agree with him when he implies that it occurred because of their "failure to establish a new function and milieu for jazz." It was enough that Parker, Gillespie, Monk, Roach and others invented a new music; as artists, they could not and should not have been asked to do more. Had they been white, most likely their achievements would have been celebrated. Being black, of course, they enjoyed no such fate. The fault, however, lay not with them, for there was no removing jazz from dingy nightclubs so long as the remainder of the society's institutions continued to operate on racist principles. The responsibility here rested with the class that controlled and still controls the institutions of the larger society; and the members of that class decided, per usual, that there were more pressing concerns than establishing a measure of equity and equality for all citizens. That the lives of so many of the bebop musicians were wasted in their prime as a result is just one more item in the long indictment against American racism. Yet Williams—with the cultural arrogance that is the hallmark of white jazz criticism—insists on blinding himself to all this. For him, it is more important to avoid the slightest taint of a social interpretation than it is to put the events of the 1940s in their proper perspective.*

---

* I remarked in chapter 1 that one of the most disturbing aspects of the work of some white critics, as here evidenced by Williams's comment on Parker's "failure," is their demonstrated readiness to pass judgment on the alleged shortcomings of "their" black subjects, without taking cognizance of the fact that there are historically conditioned personality traits that blacks have developed as a defense against a racist society. (On this subject, see, for example, Abram Kardiner and Lionel Ovesey, *The Mark of Oppression: Explorations in the Personality of the American Negro* [Cleveland: World, 1951], and William H. Grier and Price M. Cobbs, *Black Rage* [New York: Basic Books, 1968].) Vivid illustrations of this tendency in white criticism abound in, as a case in point, Joe Goldberg, *Jazz Masters of the Fifties* (New York: Macmillan, 1965), a book otherwise virtually devoid of redeeming features. Like *The Jazz Tradition*, Goldberg's volume is a series of unconnected chapters, each treating a single artist. Unlike Williams, who has sufficient intelligence to focus primarily on the music, Goldberg is obsessed with the personal idiosyncrasies of the musicians whose profiles he sketches—the Hollywood fan-magazine approach applied to jazz—and accordingly makes it a point to pass on each and every scandalous rumor. Some instances: Of Art Blakey: "when one spends time in the vicious, hothouse world that is the New York jazz scene, one hears . . . stories. Blakey lies, Blakey is a racist. Blakey caused the breakup of the original Jazz Messengers by playing Iago" (p. 57). Of Thelonious Monk: "Still he goes on his own unique way, getting in difficulties

The crowning touch with respect to Williams's book, however, is that though his hostility to Marxist interpretations is unequivocal, his reluctance to "borrow" surreptitiously the products of such an analysis is by no means so categorical. This "borrowing" emerges unmistakably in his chapter on John Coltrane when he writes:

There were times . . . in the performances with Monk and those with Davis that immediately followed them, when it seemed that, in an effort to get it all in, Coltrane was reaching for a kind

with record companies and club owners, but always remaining intractably himself" (p. 39). "Monk's natural tendency is to trust and talk to no one" (p. 41). "Those who wish to help are often rejected" (ibid.). Of Miles Davis: "Speculation on the Miles Davis character probably will go on endlessly, and countless apocryphal stories will continue to spring up" (to be repeated in books such as these, no doubt). "One may wonder what a man in his position has to be so angry about" (p. 85). Of Sonny Rollins: "The critics, whom Rollins read incessantly, were beginning to prey on his mind. He had not been successful as a leader, in his own eyes. His marriage had failed; he was drinking heavily" (p. 101). Of Cecil Taylor: "The phone rings late at night, and it is Taylor, calling from a pay booth. 'I'm around the corner,' he says. He will arrive, as likely as not, three days later" (p. 216). Of Ornette Coleman: "He now seems more bitter about those who have aided him than about his enemies. . . . This solipsistic view has led him through a rapid succession of personal managers, each of whom is replaced as Coleman feels the winds of betrayal. He once hit trumpeter Don Cherry just as they were about to go on-stage at a concert. The prices he asks for appearances are more in line with his publicity than his drawing power" (p. 241).

If it is the critic's province to traffic in trivia of this sort—a highly dubious assumption—he might at least have the decency to display a modicum of empathy in formulating his interpretations. Behavior patterns that one might consider dysfunctional if engaged in by whites could well be functional in a black context. As a case in point, the alleged abruptness or rudeness of such artists as Miles Davis and Thelonious Monk may reflect a determination to be one's own man in a society in which a black man is not supposed to be a man at all. Hence when saxophonist Steve Lacy says to Goldberg that Thelonious Monk "never does anything unless he wants to do it, and he's the only man I've ever met who really does do exactly what he wants to" (quoted, p. 32), this cries out to be understood in light of a remark by Ornette Coleman: "I thought that as long as they were white, they all had the same thing in common, to control and rule you" (quoted, p. 233). But Goldberg seems to have been more concerned with finding just the right tone of sneering derogation than with comprehending what his various sources told him.

of subdivided bop rhythm, into a sixteenth-note accent pattern. Such a thing had to be tried, and was even predictable. . . . Such a subdivided rhythm would obviously create problems in both melody and swing. . . .

From one point of view, the post-Monk Coltrane had pushed jazz harmonies as far as they could go. From another, such complex, sophisticated knowledge set its own trap, and Coltrane . . . careened around . . . in a three-dimensional harmonic maze of his own making.[25]

Now compare the above with some excerpts from an essay of mine, "Revolution, Coltrane and the Avant-Garde," that originally appeared in *Jazz* five years prior to Williams's book (July and September, 1965).[26]

One could hardly find a better example than the contrast between Coltrane's development before and after 1961 to buttress the thesis . . . that art of necessity proceeds by revolution. Although it has yet to be widely realized, what Coltrane was in actuality involved in up until that time was the attempt to carry jazz improvisation forward by a nonrevolutionary utilization of the basic bebop conventions. . . . Coltrane was as late as the end of the fifties seeking to push [the same verb Williams later used] the devices instituted by the bebop revolutionaries to their logical, evolutionary conclusion. . . .

Thus the Coltrane "sheets of sound" technique . . . must be viewed in perspective as the direct successor to the improvisations of Charlie Parker. . . . Where Parker had invoked the eighth note, Coltrane employed the sixteenth; and he similarly augmented the melodic complexity by employing more elaborate chords and a greater quantity of them.[27]

My hypothesis is that Coltrane's extension of accepted bebop practice, crystallized in the sheets of sound, had . . . just the opposite effect [from liberating the soloist]: the dense harmonic matrix and tremendously rapid speeds of execution demanded to refer to the numerous chord progressions threatened to smother the soloist beneath their combined weight. Only a supremely gifted creator—only a Coltrane, in short—could hope to negotiate this chordal straitjacket and still emerge with something of value; and in the end presumably even he found the game not worth the candle.[28]

The purpose of demonstrating Williams's use of my conclusions without attribution is least of all to convict him of plagiarism, for such "borrowing" is surely the fate of entire legions of authors. The point is rather to assert—better yet, to *prove*—that *Williams rejects the Marxian approach out of hand while at the same time appropriating for his own work ideas arrived at through an application of these same Marxist principles.* In so doing, of course, he offers the most powerful testimonial imaginable to the soundness of Marxist methodology, inveigh against it as he might. All that his polemic against Marxism can accomplish, in the final analysis, is the ultimate demonstration of the theoretical confusion of one Martin Williams. As for Marxism, its stock can only be strengthened by this tacit endorsement from one of its avowed enemies.

To avoid any confusion on this matter, it is worth spending some space demonstrating precisely how the conclusions that I reached, and that Williams repeated, flowed directly out of Marxist theory. To that end, let me try to illustrate how, in practice, one can apply such theory to concrete historical questions.

(1) *Historical development, whether in the natural universe or the social, does not take place exclusively in a smooth and continuous fashion, but is marked by abrupt discontinuities, leaps and jumps—in short, by revolutions.* Thus, jazz could not forever continue to evolve by means of gradual and continuous modifications of the basic bebop conventions. "In that respect, bebop was no different from its predecessors: beyond a certain point, continued aesthetic progress became possible solely through the wholesale demolition of the reigning paradigm—and not by successive evolutionary refinements of it."[29] Coltrane, in his "sheets of sound" period, had sought just such

an evolutionary development of bop by utilizing more chords and smaller subdivisions of the basic 4/4 pulse. His ultimate abandonment of that approach demonstrated that it was not a workable one.

(2) *The motor force behind development is conflict, struggle, antagonism, and especially contradiction.* In the case of the jazz revolution of the 1960s, the principal contradiction was between the tendency toward increased freedom for the soloist on the one hand versus the restrictions imposed by a set of regularly recurring chords in a chorus of fixed length on the other. "Viewed from one aspect, the history of jazz may be treated as the continuing (which is not to say uniform) emancipation of the soloist from the accompanying rhythmic-harmonic framework. . . . Coltrane's extension of accepted bebop practice, crystallized in the sheets of sound, had, paradoxically enough, just the opposite effect. . . ."[30] This contradiction between a longing for greater freedom and the limitations of a bebop framework—limitations that grew more stringent as the framework grew more sophisticated—was unresolvable within the existing musical conventions. A satisfactory solution was attainable solely by overthrowing those conventions—that is, by a revolution in jazz. "Nothing offers us a more direct verification of the applicability of these concepts to aesthetic revolutions than the sudden and wholly unexpected mutations in Coltrane's style that arose after he reached what quite reasonably could have been held to comprise the pinnacle of his development [the "sheets of sound"]."[31]

(3) *Changes in quantity beyond a certain point must produce corresponding changes in quality.* With respect to the jazz revolution associated with John Coltrane, we can see that a quantitative change of sufficient magnitude in the amount of freedom permitted the soloist after 1960 resulted in a qualitative change in the nature of the music. In other words, the new (post-revolutionary) music was not at all a different kind of bebop or an extension of bebop, but was instead a qualitatively different form altogether, one with its own unique rules, characteristics,

and the like. Such an abrupt transformation, by definition, comprises a revolution.

(4) A *revolutionary change transforms a thing into its dialectical opposite.* Big-band swing of the 1930s, while still synthesizing certain elements of the small-band polyphonic improvisation of the 1920s, was the dialectical opposite of it. Small-band bebop likewise was the dialectical opposite of swing (in terms of rhythm, improvising procedures, orchestra size, and so on), though nonetheless preserving various swing values (as in the music of Parker, who distilled what he needed from the work of his two major saxophone predecessors, the harmonically oriented Coleman Hawkins and the rhythmically oriented Lester Young). Finally, the jazz revolution of the 1960s went in the direction of abolishing the constraints of bebop (fixed chord sequences, for example) in order to be able to retain the gains that bebop originally had registered (primarily, its emotional intensity, as manifested in the rhythmic complexity, melodic expressiveness, and tonal qualities of Parker's playing).

In each case, a given kind of music yielded to a newer one that was its dialectical opposite, destroying the superficial aspects of the older style so that the more profound values they once had expressed might live again in a new form.[32] These successive artistic revolutions—or, more specifically, the qualities, attitudes, worldviews, and so on, that they transmit from one group of performers to their successors—are the essence of the jazz tradition. It is the task of the jazz critic, who of necessity must therefore be something of a jazz historian, to study each such dialectical revolution in the process of becoming, showing both what has been destroyed by the transformation and what, at a deeper level, has been conserved as an integral part of the tradition.[33] An author who attempts less inevitably condemns his or her work to the realm of the shallow and ephemeral.

Most white writers of books and articles on jazz, of course, have attempted less, as is woefully apparent now that courses on the history of Afro-American music have begun putting in their appearance in the college curriculum. The first problem to arise with such courses is that of finding books to assign that will be sound, historically accurate and, above all, capable of conveying what slave songs—or coon shouts, ragtime, country blues, New Orleans ensemble playing, swing, bebop, et cetera—meant to those who created and performed them. The paucity of works meeting these criteria is truly awe-inspiring—a kind of backhanded testimonial to the hegemony of white critics over black music. Martin Williams's *The Jazz Tradition* is in that sense, at any rate, aptly named, for the book does indeed represent one aspect of the jazz tradition—"You own the music and we make it" (Archie Shepp)—although not a particularly healthy one nor one that deserves to survive.

In any case, it is only too appropriate that Williams, who, by virtue of his anti-Marxist bias, renders himself unable to comprehend, still less explain, the actual, living jazz tradition, is no less confused when it comes to an understanding of what Marxism is or how its principles operate. Marxism is "unsatisfactory" because, according to Williams, it views "the complexities of man and his art as merely the transient tools of 'social forces.'"[34] One would like to know precisely how and where the author arrived at this quaint notion. One would even more like to know, however, some way in which "man and his art" might become immune to just those "social forces" that Williams is at pains to denigrate simply because Marxists recognize their historical significance. Readers for whom Marxism is synonymous with "evil" will demand no additional arguments beyond those that Williams supplies; those who prefer to think for themselves and who require more than mere ex cathedra pronouncements will not be so easily convinced. In support of his anti-Marxist position, Williams reproduces a passage from *Treat It Gentle*, the autobiography of Sidney Bechet:

> After emancipation . . . all those people who had been slaves, they needed the music more than ever now; it was like they were trying to find out in this music what they were supposed to do with this freedom: playing the music and listening to it—wait-

ing for it to express what they needed to learn once they had learned it wasn't just white people the music had to reach to, nor even to their own people, but straight out to life, and to what a man does with his life when it finally *is* his.[35]

That Williams can find in such a straightforward materialist statement of the function of music in society a confirmation of his own anti-materialist prejudices is striking evidence of the way in which one-half of a century of anti-Communist Cold Warfare has warped the thought of even those presumed to be the American intelligentsia.[36] How much longer we will have to abide such dogma is, happily, another matter. Just as the crises in American society during the 1960s moved many young historians and social scientists to reexamine the origins of the Cold War and to find its roots in the U.S. effort at the close of World War II to enforce its vision of a multilateral capitalist world order on the rest of the world, so, too, have young scholars undertaken a reinterpretation of various aspects of the black experience in history. Results of the latter have already begun to emerge, sounding notice that what the late Carter G. Woodson termed "the mis-education of the American Negro" is not going to last forever (nor, one hopes, the no less conspicuous mis-education of American whites). The sooner both of these intellectual revolutions have been consummated, the better off this country will be. If, then, Martin Williams's *The Jazz Tradition* is among the last of its kind, it will indeed have served a useful, even noble purpose.

NOTES

1. Martin Williams, *The Jazz Tradition* (New York: Oxford University Press, 1970), p. 202.
2. See LeRoi Jones (Amiri Baraka), *Black Music* (New York: William Morrow, 1968), chapter 1, pp. 11–20.
3. See Frank Kofsky, "Critiquing the Critics," chapter 1 in *Black*

Nationalism and the Revolution in Music (New York: Pathfinder Press, 1970), and also chapters 2, 3, and 8 in *John Coltrane and the Jazz Revolution of the 1960s* (New York: Pathfinder Press, 1998), the revised and expanded edition of *Black Nationalism*.

4. See André Hodeir, *Jazz: Its Evolution and Essence,* trans. David Noakes (New York: Grove Press, 1956); Gunther Schuller, *Early Jazz: Its Roots and Musical Development* (New York: Oxford University Press, 1968).

5. See LeRoi Jones, *Blues People* (New York: William Morrow, 1963) and *Black Music* (cited in full in note 2, above); A.B. Spellman, *Four Lives in the Bebop Business* (New York: Random House, 1966); Sidney Finkelstein, *Jazz: A People's Music* (New York: Citadel Press, 1948); and Francis Newton [E.J. Hobsbawm], *The Jazz Scene* (Harmondsworth, Middlesex: Penguin Books, 1961). Though they deal with another strain of black music, Charles Keil's *Urban Blues* (Chicago: University of Chicago Press, 1966), and Paul Oliver, *The Meaning of the Blues* (New York: Collier Books, 1963), also merit mention as extraordinarily perceptive social interpretations.

6. See Barry Ulanov, *A History of Jazz in America* (New York: Viking Press, 1955); Nat Hentoff, *Jazz Is* (New York: Avon Books, 1978).

7. *Jazz Tradition,* p. 8.

8. *Ibid.,* pp. 7–8.

9. *Ibid.,* p. 122.

10. *Ibid.,* p. 127.

11. The quotations from Alain Locke, *The New Negro* (New York: Atheneum, 1968), are on pp. 9, 15; those from James Weldon Johnson, *Black Manhattan* (New York: Da Capo, 1991), are on pp. 281, 284. The ambivalence of the "New Negroes" of the 1920s toward both the Garvey mass movement (which attracted its recruits primarily from the working class rather than from the middle class that spawned the artists and intellectuals) and their white peers is sensitively dissected by Robert A. Bone in Chapter 3 of *The Negro Novel in America* (New Haven: Yale University Press, 1965), "The Background of the Negro Renaissance." Gilbert Osofsky, in *Harlem: The Making of a Ghetto* (Harper & Row: New York, 1968), advances a much more somber view of Harlem life in the interwar years than that of James Weldon Johnson. The account by Elliot M. Rudwick of the *Race Riot at East St. Louis: July 2, 1917* (New York and Cleveland: Meridian, 1966) gives some idea of the savagery unleashed against blacks by whites.

12. For Gunther Schuller's observations on the first large black orchestras of the Northeast, see *Early Jazz*, p. 325.

13. James Baldwin is quoted by Richard M. Dalfiume, "The 'Forgotten Years' of the Negro Revolution," in *The Negro in Depression and War: Prelude to Revolution, 1930–1945*, ed. Bernard Sternsher (Chicago: Quadrangle, 1969), p. 299; Dalfiume's article, which deals with the World War II period, is mandatory reading for anyone with a serious interest in the social background to bebop. Black opinion on the issues raised by World War II was virtually unanimous on the hypocrisy involved in having a nation whose capital was segregated by law pose as the leader of an ostensibly antiracist and democratic crusade. As Roy Wilkins pointedly observed, "It sounds pretty foolish to be against park benches marked 'Jude' [Jew] in Berlin, but for park benches marked 'Colored' in Tallahassee, Florida." Quoted in *White Racism: Its History, Pathology and Practice*, eds. Barry N. Schwartz and Robert Disch (New York: Laurel-Dell, 1971), p. 47.

14. Francis Newton [E.J. Hobsbawm], *The Jazz Scene*, pp. 203–04.

15. Leslie B. Rout, Jr., "Reflections on the Evolution of Post-War Jazz," *Negro Digest*, XVIII:4 (February 1969), pp. 92–93

16. Newton [Hobsbawm], *The Jazz Scene*, p. 207.

17. Ira Gitler, "Ira Gitler to Frank Kofsky," letter to the editor in *Jazz*, July 1965, pp. 6–7. See Kofsky, *John Coltrane and the Jazz Revolution of the 1960s*, chapter 1, for a more-detailed recounting of the dispute among Gitler, myself, and others over the correct interpretation of the bebop revolution.

18. Ross Russell, *Bird Lives! The High Life and Hard Times of Charlie (Yardbird) Parker* (New York: Charterhouse, 1973), pp. 151–52; see also pp. 96, 118, 140–41, 209 for more material on Parker's overt resistance to racism. An even better source of information on this score is Robert G. Reisner, *Bird: The Legend of Charlie Parker* (New York: Citadel, 1962); for representative instances of Parker's opposition to racism, see the narratives of Teddy Blume and Duke Jordan, pp. 61–62 and 126, respectively. Reisner's work remains, in my opinion, the single most valuable source on Parker.

19. Art Blakey's description of this incident is in Reisner, *Bird*, p. 51; see also Russell, *Bird Lives*, pp. 159–60.

20. See Jones, *Blues People*, pp. 199–200.

21. See Williams, *Jazz Tradition*, pp. 136–37.

22. See, for example, *ibid.*, p. 136.

23. See Finkelstein, *Jazz*, pp. 266–70; the second quotation is on p. 269.

24. *Ibid.*, p. 270.

25. *Jazz Tradition*, pp. 200–01.

26. Frank Kofsky, "Revolution, Coltrane and the Avant-Garde," *Jazz*, July and September 1965; reprinted, with some revisions, as "John Coltrane and the Revolution in Black Music," in *John Coltrane and the Jazz Revolution of the 1960s*.

27. "Revolution, Coltrane and the Avant-Garde," *Jazz*, July 1965, p. 16.

28. "Revolution, Coltrane and the Avant-Garde," *Jazz*, September 1965, p. 19.

29. *Ibid.*

30. *Ibid.*, pp. 18–19.

31. *Ibid.*, p. 19.

32. I develop these points at greater length in chapter 10 of *John Coltrane and the Jazz Revolution of the 1960s*.

33. For one effort at applying this approach to the revolutionary procedures developed by John Coltrane and Elvin Jones, see chapter 10 in *John Coltrane and the Jazz Revolution of the 1960s*. Incidentally, it was in response to an earlier version of that same essay that J.R. Taylor, Martin Williams's assistant at the Smithsonian Institution, attempted to intimidate the editorial board of *The Journal of Jazz Studies* from publishing any further work of mine (Taylor's letter appears above as the epigraph to chapter 5). In such fashion did the distinguished scholars of the Smithsonian Institution's jazz program encourage freedom of intellectual inquiry and discussion.

34. *Jazz Tradition*, p. 10.

35. Bechet quoted in *ibid.*, p. 14.

36. If Williams fails to understand Marxism correctly, he fails no less signally in understanding what the blues is about. Marxists, he writes, "will find precious little confirmation" for their interpretation of black music "in the lyrics to traditional blues," since these "deal far more often with the problems of courtship, personal morality, and natural forces—storms, floods—than with society" (*Jazz Tradition*, p. 9). This is, of course, the sheerest nonsense—and on several counts, at that. How, for instance, can the "problems of courtship" and "personal morality" be said to exist apart from "society," or, rather, the "place" of black people in society? Are not patterns of courtship among blacks socially conditioned? Are not standards of "personal morality" the same? Did not many of both have their origins in the conditions of slavery? Moreover, as Paul

Oliver has shown in his seminal work on the interpretation of blues lyrics, *The Meaning of the Blues,* either that music is to be comprehended through a social perspective or it is not to be comprehended at all. Blues, Oliver cogently remarks (p. 32), "had meaning not only for the singer but for every Negro who listened. In the blues were reflected the effects of the economic stress on the depleted plantations and the unexpected prosperity of the urban centers where conditions of living still could not improve. In the blues were to be found the major catastrophes both personal and national, the triumphs and miseries that were shared by all, yet private to one. In the blues were reflected the family disputes, the upheavals caused by poverty [anti-Marxists, please take note!] and migration, the violence and bitterness, the tears and the happiness of all. In the blues an unsettled, unwanted people during these periods of social unrest found the security, the unity and the strength that it so desperately desired."

7

The Afro-American folk roots
of innovation in jazz

In the first edition of *Black Nationalism and the Revolution in Music*,[1] I attempted to analyze the notion that "anyone" can learn to play jazz. As part of that analysis, I proposed that, for non-black musicians, mastery of the jazz idiom could be looked upon as analogous to

> learning to express oneself in a foreign tongue. While it is always a theoretical possibility that an author can develop as a major voice in a language not his own, nonetheless the fact remains that very few in the history of literature have been able to accomplish this feat.[2]

Hence the "most obvious explanation for the continued domination of all the various . . . [jazz] polls by black artists" is that "black youth do, after all, grow up in an environment in which Afro-American music of all sizes and shapes . . . is ubiquitous." Accordingly, in his or her development as a jazz musician, a black "youngster has an inestimable cultural advantage over the white youth who is not continuously exposed to the same musical fare." One can also infer the importance of an early exposure to the Afro-American musical tradition by noting the innovators whose contributions to jazz have been the most profound and lasting, for "if we were to compile the names of the ten or twenty-five or fifty most significant jazz artists, those whose ideas have had the greatest influence on contemporary and subsequent generations, the color of such a list, so to speak, would be overwhelmingly black."[3]

In this chapter, then, I will provide and examine a concrete example that illustrates in detail how the social environment confers advantages with respect to the playing of Afro-American music on a black youth while withholding those advantages from a white. I will also explore the significance for the writing of black history of mechanisms that people of African descent in North America have evolved in order to preserve those aspects of culture that they themselves regard as paramount.

The writers and scholars, mostly white but some black as well, who have sought to narrate the history of black people in the United States have, to my way of thinking, too often been guilty of operating with a perspective made overly narrow by ethnocentric and/or class biases. Thus, as music and dance usually are peripheral to the concerns and way of life of most white (and even some black) middle- or upper-class academicians, the latter automatically and rather too hastily have tended to assume that music and dance were equally marginal in the lives of Africans who were enslaved and brought to this country against their wills. Because they view political and economic institutions as having greater significance than those revolving around music and dance, the academics dogmatically assert, without giving the matter the scrutiny it deserves, that African peoples underwent the stripping away of the "really important" aspects of their culture—that is, their political and economic systems—when they were carried as slaves to North America, leaving them with "merely" their traditions pertaining to music, dance, and perhaps religion. From this point it is but a short step to the deduction that chattel slavery in the United States was so "total" an institution that it methodically "depersonalized" and "infantilized" each of its victims into a passive, robot-like nullity—a zombie, as it were, or to be more precise, a stereotypical "Sambo."[4]

An investigation conducted less along a priori lines and with greater regard for both evidence and its interpretation would, in contrast, point to radically different conclusions. With respect to innovation in jazz specifically, it is immediately pertinent to note the absolutely central role played by music in the lives of Africans as well as African-descended peoples. In his study, *Negro Folk Music, U.S.A.*, for instance, the anthropologist Harold Courlander remarks that "music permeated virtually every important phase of living in Africa, from birth to death." In the same vein, elsewhere he notes that

> from northwestern Africa to the Cape, the African tends to think of music as heard action, and of any silent rhythmical activity as an echo of music. Singing, and sometimes percussive effects, customarily accompanies the cutting of trees, the clearing of brush, the hoeing of fields, the hoisting of sails, the hauling of a hawser, the pounding of grain in a mortar, and the winnowing of rice. An individual working alone at such tasks may depend upon singing to complete his physical activity.

A laborer in South Africa thus told Courlander that the work couldn't be performed without musical accompaniment: "Without singing we have no strength." In Nigeria, a woodcutter explained that "if the trees are to be cut, you must sing. Without a song the bush knife is dull." Significantly, Courlander heard similar remarks among African-Americans, for example, the comment of an Alabama track-liner: "Man, singing just naturally makes the work go easier. If you didn't have singing you wouldn't get hardly anything out of these men."[5]

In his groundbreaking monograph, *Early Jazz,* Gunther Schuller underscores this point even more emphatically, in a passage that again calls our attention to the cultural continuities between Africans and Afro-Americans:

> African native music and early American jazz both originate in a total vision of life, in which music, unlike the art music of Europe, is not a separate, autonomous social domain. . . . In so far as it has not been influenced by European or American customs, African music even today has no separate abstracted function. It is not surprising that the word "art" does not even exist in African languages. Nor does the African divide art into separate categories. Folklore, music, dance, sculpture, and painting operate as a total generic unit, serving not only religion *but all phases of daily life, encompassing birth, death, work, and play* [my italics].

It is, moreover, Schuller's view, based upon a painstaking sifting of the evidence, that in the United States "these African traditions survive in an astonishing array of musical detail."[6]

The research of Courlander, Schuller, and others confirms that, unlike the case with middle-class white academics and professionals, music and dance for Africans and Afro-Americans are not activities that are easily divorced from the routine of daily existence, but instead comprise a vital component of, and accompaniment to, all aspects of that existence. Of the numerous consequences that flow from this conclusion, the most important for our purposes have to do with the high value that African and African-descended peoples attach to the ability to be completely responsive to music and dance. The foregoing evidence from the works of Courlander and Schuller, as well as my own to be introduced presently, strongly suggests that no person of African ancestry would be considered by the community to be a fully developed human being unless he or she were able to demonstrate a thorough grounding in the communal customs of music and dance. That is to say, to a person raised according to the precepts of African culture, a well-honed sensitivity to the nuances of music and the expressive motions of dance would be about as integral and crucial in adult life as is, say, the possession of literacy to the person reared in a contemporary Western European culture. In each instance, without the particular skills involved, a person lacking them would necessarily be excluded from large and essential areas of the culture—so much so as to make that person a virtual "foreigner" in his or her native land.

Even a cursory examination of the means they have developed for instructing their youth in the music- and dance-related folkways of the community supplies strong evidence that peoples of African descent do indeed place great emphasis on the role of music and dance in the life of the typical adult. For if it is something of a truism that a community will devise both formal and informal methods for socializing its youth in all areas of knowledge and behavior that it deems significant, conversely, we may reasonably infer that where such patterns of socialization can be shown to exist, they have come into being to preserve and transmit aspects of the cultural legacy that the community regards as essential.

We can at once apply this line of reasoning to a specific instance that dates from the time of slavery, namely, that of "clapping Juba" and its twentieth-century descendant, the "Hambone" game. Juba, a competitive or challenge dance of African origins ("in Africa this dance was called the *Djouba*"[7]), has been described by several nineteenth-century observers in the slave-plantation regions of the Caribbean and United States: In the United States, where masters usually did not allow use of drums, the slaves provided a percussive accompaniment by "patting Juba"—that is, by stamping, clapping, slapping of palms against each other and on arms, chest, thighs, and even the face. (This fact, incidentally, indicates the profound silliness of the notion propounded by many historians that the masters were successful in suppressing certain features of the African culture of the slaves simply by prohibiting the drum.*) One of the best and clearest accounts of patting Juba has come down to us from the pen of a person who was himself a slave, Solomon Northup. In his autobiographical account, *Twenty Years a Slave*, Northup recounted that the dancing of the slaves did not necessarily

> cease with the sound of the fiddle, but in that case they [slaves] set up a music peculiar to themselves. This is called "patting," accompanied with one of those unmeaning songs, composed rather for its adaptation to a certain tune or measure, than for the purpose of expressing any distinct idea. The patting is performed by striking the hands on the knees, then striking the hands together, then striking the right shoulder with one hand, the left with the other—all the while keeping time with the feet, and singing. . . .[8]

Although the Juba dance itself is probably no longer performed as such within the United States, the practice of "patting Juba" apparently survives to the present era as one component of a game bearing the name "the Hambone." In all fundamentals of clapping, slapping, foot-tapping, accompaniment with nonsense rhymes, and so forth, patting Juba does not seem to have changed substantially since the days of slavery. Two of my informants in this connection, Messrs. Les Pogue and Norman Harris, performed a demonstration of the Hambone in my classes in the History of Black Music in America. Both men stated that, as youths, they had played versions of the Hambone game as late as the 1950s, in places as widely separated as Boston (Harris) and Wichita Falls, Texas (Pogue); Les

---

* Historians seem consistently to have underestimated the resourcefulness of enslaved Afro-Americans. In a performance in Davis, California, in May 1972, for instance, the Georgia Sea Island Singers drew on the same methods of rhythmic accompaniment (clapping, stamping, slapping arms, legs, et cetera) as slaves employed in "clapping Juba," and, moreover, supplied additional percussion by beating wooden planks together or against the floor. One can wager that this practice did not originate in Davis in a.d. 1972!

Pogue also recalled that young black men competed for cash prizes in the Hambone contests that were a feature of the traveling medicine shows then touring the Southwestern United States—contests clearly analogous to the "cutting sessions" at one time conducted by jazz musicians.[9] More recently, another version of the Hambone game has been set down on record by that indefatigable chronicler of black folk culture, Taj Mahal.[10]

The survival of the constellation of body movements and rhythms that together constitute patting Juba and the Hambone game can, if we interpret it properly, tell us a great deal about black people and their culture. To begin with, the mere fact that these movements and rhythms have been for so long preserved as a part of black folklore argues, as I indicated earlier, that the social priorities and values of the black community cannot be assumed to be those of middle-class white academicians. To be more precise, black people attach greater importance than do whites to, among other things, the acquisition of a sophisticated rhythmic sensibility. This is further evidenced by the evolution of patting Juba from an adult activity to a game whose hidden content, or function, is the socialization of black youth so as to produce in them just that highly developed responsiveness to rhythmic music that is particularly prized within the black community. For generally speaking, the attitudes, beliefs, and especially skills that are transmitted to children and youth via such apparently innocuous and even seemingly purposeless "games" as the Hambone often turn out, on closer inspection, to be among those deemed most important within the culture. Given what we can learn from them about the values held by black people, then, these games are surely deserving of more careful scrutiny than the nearly complete neglect they have thus far received in the conventional histories of Afro-America.[11]

Second, if we consider the high priority placed upon musical responsiveness in African or African-derived cultures together with the demonstrated ability of Afro-Americans to maintain and transmit to subsequent generations the dominant musical elements of that culture—as illustrated by the retention of the

African *Djouba* dance and its later transformation into patting Juba and then the Hambone game—if we consider these two phenomena in concert, it is clear that any notion of the "depersonalization," the "infantilization," the "Sambo-ization" of black people enslaved in the United States has to be abandoned. Because if proficiency in music, dance, and related activities has the significance for African peoples that the evidence suggests, and if these cultural attributes have for the most part been retained, as the evidence also suggests, then there can be no basis whatsoever for speculations that depict Afro-Americans as having been denuded of their culture by the admittedly corrosive experiences of chattel slavery. As has long been apparent to those with even a smattering of knowledge of Afro-American music and dance in relationship to African, a people who had been genuinely "depersonalized," and so forth, would not have the capability shown by black people here to preserve intact such large and enormously vital aspects of their cultural heritage.[12] The problem, of course, has been that heretofore historians have been unwilling to confront black music and dance with complete intellectual objectivity; rather, they have predetermined the outcome of their research by refusing to confer on music and dance the same importance ascribed to them by the African-descended peoples whose history they were ostensibly engaged in writing. This untenable procedure can no longer be justified on any rational, unbiased grounds, and one hopes that it will soon become wholly obsolete.[13]

My next point concerns the question that originally occasioned this discussion of patting Juba and the Hambone—to wit, the advantages with respect to jazz creativity that an upbringing within the black community confers. The hypothesis I advanced earlier is that, having already unconsciously absorbed the leading elements of the Afro-American musical tradition, a black youth is considerably more advanced in his jazz studies than would be a white youth of comparable age and raw ability; hence the former is by the same token much better prepared to essay the role of musical innovator within jazz. We can turn to the Hambone game for a specific illustration of this process at work. In essence, the game consists of producing a series of variations on a highly syncopated, rapidly executed pattern of sixteenth notes, reminiscent of motifs found ubiquitously in current soul music as well as in some earlier black music forms (such as gospel). For instance:

To be able to create, or for that matter even grasp, this extremely fast rhythm requires that the participants—including the onlookers, who sometimes function as formal or informal judges of the competition—develop the ability to handle complex sequences of (syncopated) accents that alternate irregularly between the beats and the off-beats. In the above example, for instance, the *ands* of the first and third beats are so heavily accented that at times they appear to *become* those beats. The going can get even stickier yet when, as is frequently the case, there is more than a single person producing the Hambone rhythm, for in that event the syncopations of a single performer are replaced by even more dense and complicated rhythms reminiscent of African drumming. Naturally, the apprenticeship provided by the Hambone game and other rhythmic socialization activities of young black people is a superb preparation for the playing of jazz (or any form of black music), inasmuch as the jazz musician must constantly have recourse to such syncopations and rhythmic complexity as means of investing improvised solos with interest and unpredictability. Where a white musician may be able to master the use of syncopations and polyrhythmic patterns only after considerable struggle—the difficulties symphonic string players encounter with jazz phrasing are notorious in this regard—many a black musician will be able to phrase on and off the beat, with and "against" the rhythm, without giving the matter so much as a second thought. And this, I would stress, is an ability that is at the very *heart* of jazz performance.

The Hambone game (as well as others like it) is also important because it teaches the performers what jazz drummers refer to as "independence"—that is, the ability to execute simultaneous cross-rhythms with both arms, both legs, the head and the torso. Such coordinated but autonomous polyrhythmic body movements are an absolute prerequisite for creating jazz music on the percussion instruments, including the piano, drums (witness the work of Elvin Jones and Anthony Williams especially), vibraharp, et cetera. But as anyone who has even a casual acquaintanceship with it must have observed, movements of this nature are also an integral and fundamental aspect of black dance. It would thus appear that there is a relationship—difficult to specify with complete precision, but real nonetheless—between socialization games like the Hambone on the one hand and the motor skills necessary for participating in black dance or the playing of black music on the other. Perhaps we can best summarize this relationship with the statement that the Hambone game, like other rhythmic socialization activities, provides black youth with a set of abilities that in adult life can be applied either to black music and/or black dance, depending on the desires of the individual.[14]

Socialization activities along the lines of the Hambone game make it clear why virtually all of the major innovations in jazz have been the product of black creativity. Instead of having to learn the basic rhythmic and melodic vocabulary as does a white performer, a black artist is free to concentrate talent and energy on refining, enriching, and perfecting that vocabulary by a manipulation and extension of fundamental concepts. We should also keep in mind in this context that socialization devices like the Hambone game are unique to black people. As Harold Courlander explains,

> handclapping as accompaniment to singing is found in many cultures, but although occasionally used, it is not a standard fix-

ture in non-Negro settings in the United States. On the other hand, it is normally present in the children's songs, playparty songs [of which the Hambone is one] and certain types of religious songs in the Negro West Indies and is apparent that this musical device is of African derivation.[15]

Hence despite the fact that jazz music has been relatively widely disseminated on a world scale during the last few decades, it does *not* follow, as some have rather naively argued, that now "anyone" can aspire to become a jazz *innovator* (as opposed to a competent jazz *musician*). For although the easy availability of jazz recordings will certainly operate to reduce the cultural advantages of black youth to a degree, the evidence I have presented here strongly suggests that mere exposure to jazz recordings alone will not extinguish that advantage altogether. It is not simply because they have heard more jazz recordings during their childhood and youth that black artists have been far and away the dominant innovators in jazz. Rather, it is because they are immersed in a social milieu that is itself suffused with the complex rhythmic juxtapositions, syncopations, cadences, timbres, body movements, and so on, of African-based music and dance—and this fact is not about to change. For the foreseeable future, in which the destruction of de facto separation of white and black communities appears at best a remote possibility, we can anticipate that black artists will continue to be the source of the leading innovations in jazz.

The ability of the black community to retain, through such devices as games of socialization, the fundamental constituents of the African musical heritage—a retention that Gunther Schuller, for one, lavishly documents in the first chapter of *Early Jazz*—supplies us with an explanation for the preponderance of black artists among the outstanding innovators in jazz; it explains as well an otherwise puzzling fact on which a number of observers have commented. In the words of anthropologist and blues scholar Charles Keil, "in every instance" in which a new style of black music has been created, "the new music has been an amalgamation of increased musical knowledge (technically speaking) and a reemphasis of the most basic Afro-American resources." Keil observes, by way of illustration, that "Elvin Jones and the other percussion virtuosos of contemporary jazz" have, "in attempting to create a maximum amount of swing, . . . inevitably worked toward the crossed triplet rhythms of West Africa."[16] Yet it should be obvious that no such calling upon "the most basic resources" of African or African-derived music could ever take place if the black community had not previously forged methods of preserving and transmitting these resources. If the components of a tradition are to remain available to provide the building blocks of successive waves of innovation, then, it is incontestable that some means of ensuring the survival of that tradition must first be devised.

Heretofore, however, as I remarked earlier, historians, even those who specialize in the history of black music, generally have not bothered to search for the precise mechanisms by which essential aspects of the African musical tradition have been kept intact. As a result, they are often at a loss to explain exactly how innovations that increase the African, rather than the European, content of black American music come about. Gunther Schuller offers us a striking case in point. Noting "the African" either "thinks in eighth notes or, if he is momentarily thinking in quarter notes, is capable of feeling the eighth-note subdivisions just as strongly," this fact leads Schuller

> to the interesting speculation whether the penchant in "modern jazz" to feel the eighth note as a basic time unit is in any way related to African music. It is certainly clear by now that one of Charlie Parker's most enduring innovations was precisely this splitting of the four beats in a bar into eight.

So far, good enough. But, lacking a firm empirical basis for understanding the continuity between African music and Parker's innovations, Schuller soon wanders onto a treacherous path. "Was this," he asks, "like the emergence of some underground river, the musical reincarnation of impulses subconsciously remembered from generations earlier . . . ?"[17] By the latter phrase Schuller evidently intends the notion of a "racial memory" in the Jungian sense, for subsequently, having converted his originally shaky hypothesis into an even more dubious postulate, he explicitly asserts that "the same polyrhythmic character [that] African music has" is "transmitted through racial memory into jazz."[18]

But by now it should be evident that one need not resort to bizarre schemes that depend on "racial memory" when far less fanciful ideas can account for the ability of Charlie Parker, Elvin Jones, and countless other black artists to draw upon elements of the African musical legacy in working out their own pioneering concepts. The survival of these elements in games of socialization such as the Hambone (which, like both African music and Charlie Parker's improvisations, is built on an eighth-note pulse), and in other forms as well, shows clearly how this tradition is preserved at the folk level until black musical innovators need to make use of it; wild and ungrounded speculations about alleged "racial memory," besides opening the door to the construction of racist ideologies based on the presumed contents of such "memories," are therefore wholly gratuitous. The continued availability in folk forms of these elements should dispel any lingering mystery about how one group of musicians after another can invoke them to generate jazz innovations— innovations that have the effect of heightening the African attributes of the music rather than increasing its European ones. Inasmuch as black musicians do, by virtue of their youthful socialization by the community, have greater access to this African cultural background, it is only to be expected that they would also be the source of the most compelling innovations. It is, after all, *their* heritage from which the music has sprung, and, accordingly, every additional exposure to the myriad aspects of the African musical tradition can only enhance their ability to reshape and redirect it.

In this chapter I have argued for the view that jazz not only arose from black origins, but that, because of the segregated nature of American society, in which the great majority of black and white youth develop along divergent cultural and psychological paths, it has to this moment remained tied to these origins and gives no evidence of being about to change.* Only when we have fully recognized this continuous grounding of jazz in the Afro-American folk tradition will we be able to account for the nature of the most recent innovations in this music and the fact that they, like nearly all of the most noteworthy advances, have been fashioned by black artists. Perhaps by then we will have come to appreciate the historical significance of the fact that these black creators, cut off though they are from the land of their ancestors by almost two centuries, are nonetheless still in touch with the cultural heritage brought here and maintained by men and women who may have been enslaved, but were anything but passive recipients of the mores that their European-American owners sought to instill in them.

---

* Dexter Gordon's biography is exemplary in this respect. At age thirteen his father gave him his first instrument, a clarinet. "I didn't know anything about making music," he has recalled, "*but the knowledge that I had in my head was really broad; my thing [style] was already forming* [my italics]. I was listening to all the bands, everybody I could, and I'd go around where the cats were, when the bands came into town, and I'd carry somebody's horn into the dance. Later on, I would let Sonny Rollins and Jackie McLean do the same thing for me, when they were kids. I knew where they were, 'cause I'd done the same thing myself" (Gordon is quoted in Pete Hamill's notes to *Dexter Gordon Quartet: Manhattan Symphonie* [Columbia JC 356 DTY]). Probably not one white youth in ten thousand had the opportunity to enjoy the kind of early musical experiences afforded Gordon, Rollins, and McLean.

NOTES

1. Frank Kofsky, *Black Nationalism and the Revolution in Music* (New York: Pathfinder, 1970).

2. *Ibid.*, p. 16.

3. *Ibid.*, pp. 16–19 *passim*.

4. This is a schematic restatement of the well-known but now largely discredited thesis of Stanley Elkins, *Slavery: A Problem in American Institutional and Intellectual Life* (Chicago: University of Chicago Press, 1959).

5. Harold Courlander, *Negro Folk Music, U.S.A.* (New York and London: Columbia University Press, 1963), pp. 38, 90–91.

6. Gunther Schuller, *Early Jazz: Its Roots and Musical Development* (New York: Oxford University Press, 1968), pp. 4–5, 6.

7. For a discussion of Caribbean and U.S. versions of the Juba dance, see Lynne F. Emery, *Black Dance: In the United States from 1619 to 1970* (Palo Alto, California: National Press, 1972), pp. 27–29, 96–98; the quotation is from p. 96.

8. Solomon Northup, *Twenty Years a Slave,* in Gilbert Osofsky, ed., *Puttin' On Ole Massa* (New York: Harper & Row, 1961), pp. 345–46; see also p. 385. *Cf.* the following description of "accompanists who 'patted' with the hands, keeping accurate time with the music. In patting, the position was usually a halfstoop or forward bend, with a slap of one hand on the left knee followed by the same stroke and noise on the right, and then a loud slap of the two palms together. I should add that the left hand made two strokes in half-time to one for the right, something after the double stroke of the left drumstick in beating the kettledrum." Dr. John Wyeth, a Huntsville, Alabama, plantation owner, quoted in Emery, *Black Dance,* pp. 96–97.

9. Les Pogue and Norman Harris, tape-recorded class presentation, California State University, Sacramento, February 23, 1972. Pogue adds that in 1962 he was stationed in London by the U.S. Army, where he had an opportunity to frequent nightclubs favored by Ghanians, Kenyans, Jamaicans, and other black people in that city. Here, to his surprise, he witnessed and participated in a type of rhythmic activity that was, to him, obviously related to the Hambone game; the major difference was that the rhythms were created on drums rather than by slapping parts of the body. See also Emery, *Black Dance,* p. 98. I am grateful to Les Pogue,

Norman Harris, and the several other students who assisted me in gaining information on rhythm games played by black young people.

10. Taj Mahal, "A Little Soulful Tune," *De Ole Folks At Home/Giant Step* (Columbia GP 18).

11. As probably goes without saying, the anthropologists have a much superior record in the matter of interpreting various aspects of black culture, including games of socialization. For representative studies of language socialization games, see, for example, Robert D. Abrahams, *Deep Down in the Jungle: Negro Narrative Folklore from the Streets of Philadelphia* (Chicago: Aldine Publishing, 1970), and Thomas Kochman, "Toward an Ethnography of Black American Speech Behavior," in Norman E. Whitten, Jr., and John F. Szwed, eds., *Afro-American Anthropology: Contemporary Perspectives* (New York: The Free Press, 1970), pp. 145–62.

12. Gunther Schuller, for example, states that "It is . . . evident that many more aspects of jazz derive directly from African musical-social traditions than has been assumed. . . . The analytic study in this chapter [Chapter 1, "The Origins"] shows that every musical element—rhythm, harmony, melody, timbre and the basic forms of jazz—is essentially African in background and derivation. . . . Acculturation took place, *but only to the extent that the Negro allowed European elements to become integrated into his African heritage* [my emphasis]. . . . Thus one can say that within the loose framework of European tradition, the American Negro was able to preserve a significant nucleus of his African heritage." Such an achievement in the face of utmost adversity is scarcely what one would expect from a cultural "Sambo" or zombie. See Schuller, *Early Jazz*, p. 62. In similar fashion, Paul Oliver, *Savannah Syncopators: African Retentions in the Blues* (New York: Stein and Day, 1970), has established the African origins not only of the blues as music, but even of the very *instruments* upon which that body of music has been created. The reader should also consult Emery, *Black Dance,* for yet another set of reinforcing conclusions drawn from research in a different field. Unfortunately for the state of historical scholarship, however, most historians have in practice felt entirely free to disregard the implications of such findings at their pleasure. My suggestion is that graduate schools in history would be well advised to drop the requirements for reading knowledge of two non-English languages and substitute (at least for one) courses in comparative musicology and African dance; it may become more essential for historians studying Afro-American history to be able to take apart a pattern of syncopated sixteenth notes,

say, than to commit to memory the conjugation of certain irregular French verbs.

13. A process that has in fact already started in the work of some scholars. A model in this regard is Lawrence Levine's skillful and perceptive use of spirituals to show that African-American slaves rejected prevailing white racist beliefs about their nature and capacities and instead defiantly asserted in song their own humanity, self-esteem, and refusal to accept bondage as their "natural" and permanent fate. See Levine, *Black Culture and Black Consciousness: Afro-American Folk Thought from Slavery to Freedom* (New York: Oxford University Press, 1977). Two other rewarding works that supplement Levine are Sterling Stuckey, "Through the Prism of Folklore: The Black Ethos in Slavery," *The Massachusetts Review*, IX:3 (Summer 1968), pp. 417–37; and James H. Cone, *The Spirituals and the Blues: An Interpretation* (New York: Seabury Press, 1972).

14. To date, white musicians seem to have made greatest inroads in jazz on two instruments, piano and bass (several of Charlie Parker's pianists, for example, were white). It seems to me that the coordinated independence of hand (and to a lesser extent, foot) movements that any successful pianist is forced to develop is probably in a rough way analogous to the coordinated independence acquired in the course of mastering such black socialization games as the Hambone; hence a thoroughly schooled white pianist already is able to command the basic motor abilities (if not necessarily the concepts) that will allow him or her to play the syncopations and rhythmic juxtapositions that are an essential element of jazz and, indeed, all black music. As for the bass, my intuition here is that white jazz bassists benefit in their youth from the characteristic preoccupation of European-descended peoples with the (bowed) string instruments that comprise the dominant component of the symphonic orchestra; whereas the playing of the reed and brass instruments most often heard in jazz—saxophone, trumpet, trombone—is by comparison neglected.

15. *Negro Folk Music*, p. 28. My interest in hand-clapping and other modes of black rhythmic socialization was first aroused by Cliff and Julia Houdek, who pointed out to me that the patterns clapped by black and white children were vastly different, those of the former being enormously more complex by virtue of their highly syncopated and rhythmically subdivided nature. (By "rhythmically subdivided," I mean that where white children usually clap quarter-note patterns, black children

will invariably subdivide the quarter notes into quarter-note triplets, eighth notes, eighth-note triplets, sixteenth notes, and so forth.)

16. Charles Keil, *Urban Blues* (Chicago: University of Chicago Press, 1966), pp. 43, 45. As another case in point, the "Bo Diddley" rhythmic pattern that first made its appearance in black popular music during the 1950s (in the work of Ellas McDaniel, "Bo Diddley," who gave that rhythm its name) can be traced directly back to African antecedents (to the best of my knowledge, it does not occur with any frequency or prominence in European art music). See by way of example the recording by Alhaji Bai Konte, *Kora Melodies from the Republic of Gambia, West Africa* (Rounder Records 5001), especially the selection "Alla l'aa ke." I am grateful to Julie Blattler for bringing this piece of music to my attention in my class on the History of Black Music in America.

17. Schuller, *Early Jazz*, p. 25.

18. *Ibid.*, p. 293.

APPENDIX A

*Mark Levine's contract
with Catalyst Records*

C A T A L Y S T   R E C O R D S

S T A N D A R D

A R T I S T   A G R E E M E N T

AGREEMENT made this 22 day of July, 1976
by and between CATALYST RECORDS, Los Angeles, California, and/or
its associates, subsidiaries, nominees, successors and assignees
(hereinafter referred to as the "Company") and _____

_____ MARK LEVINE _____

_____, professionally known as

_____, (hereinafter

referred to as "Artist").

W I T N E S S E T H

WHEREAS, the Company is engaged in the business of manu-
facturing, producing, recording, selling and distributing phonograph records; and

WHEREAS, the Artist is a musician;

NOW, THEREFORE, in consideration of the mutual promises
herein contained, and other good and valuable consideration, re-
ceipt and sufficiency whereof is hereby acknowledged, the parties
hereto agree as follows:

1. That the Artist will render his exclusive personal
services during the term hereof for the recording and making of
phonograph records at such studios as the Company may designate,
at times and places to be mutually agreed upon by and between the
parties hereto. Should the Artist for any reason be unavailable
for rendering such services, the term of this agreement shall, at
the Company's option, be automatically extended for such period
of time as the Artists shall have been unavailable. All such extensions of the period of this agreement shall apply consecutively
to the end of the term of the particular period in which such
failure to record occurs. The dates, therefore, for the exercise
of subsequent options and the dates for the commencement of the
renewal terms thereof shall accordingly be extended. The Company
shall notify the Artist of all such extensions and the limiting
dates thereof, by registered mail, at least fifteen (15) days
prior to the original termination date of the period during which
such failure of the Artist to make himself available occurs.

The musical compositions to be recorded shall be selected
by the Company and the recordings shall be subject to the approval
of the Company as satisfactory as to the quality and commercial
value for the manufacture and sale as phonograph records and tapes.
The Artist will perform for the recording of a minimum number of
records hereinafter set forth. Additional recordings, over and
above the minimum number hereinafter specified shall be performed
by the Artist and recorded by the Company at the election of the
Company. The Artist agrees to re-record each selection to be
made hereunder until commercially satisfactory "master" record
thereof shall have been obtained. In the event that during the
term of this agreement, or during any option period, the Company,
with the Artist's consent, records more than the minimum number
of record sides required to be recorded in such period as provided for herein, then such sides as may be recorded in excess
of said minimum may be applied, at Company's sole option, to reduce the minimum number of record sides required to be recorded
during any subsequent period.

2. During the term of this agreement of any extension
or extensions thereof, the Artist will not perform for the purpose of making phonograph records or tapes for any person, firm,

-1-

or corporation other than the Company, and the Artist acknow-
ledges that the Artist's services are unique and extraordinary
and the Company shall be entitled to equitable and injunctive
relief to enforce the provisions of this paragraph, in addition
to any other available remedies.

3. The Company shall specify and pay the costs of the
Artist's accompaniment, instrumental arrangements, copying and
studio costs, in connection with performances hereunder; and all
such costs shall be charged against the Artist's royalties. Without limiting the generality of the foregoing, also included among
costs or payments which the Company shall be entitled to charge
against the Artist's royalties under this or any other agreement
between the parties hereto, if and whom earned, shall be any and
all amounts which are paid by the Company pursuant to the requirements of any collective bargaining agreement, trust agreement, or
any other agreement between the Company and any union, guild, or
association representing the Artist or other persons who render
services hereunder, or in connection with any accompaniment
(instrumental and vocal), arrangements and copying for performances hereunder, whether received by the Artist or such persons
or paid directly to the union, guild, association, or trustee,
and whether or not such amounts are related to, based upon or
computed by reference to union scale payments for services rendered by the Artist or such persons, providing that said payments
are due either as a result of recordings hereunder or the manufacture and/or sale of phonograph records and/or tapes embodying
performances hereunder.

4. The Company agrees to pay the Artist for the
services rendered hereunder:

(a) A royalty of_SIX_(6%) percent of the retail
selling price (less all taxes and packaging costs) of
ninety percent (90%) of all phonograph records embodying on both sides thereof the compositions performed
by the Artist and recorded hereunder, manufactured,
sold and paid for, and not returned, other than those
records given away or sold by the Company at approximately the cost of production or advertising purposes.

(b) One-half (1/2) of the preceding amount of ninety
percent (90%) of all phonograph records embodying such
composition(s) on only one side thereof, so manufactured,
sold and paid for and not returned.

(c) With respect to a long-playing (33 1/3 rpm) or
extended play (45 rpm) microgroove record which embodies
compositions in addition to the composition(s) performed
by the Artist and recorded hereunder, royalties shall be
computed upon that fraction of the selling price as the
number of recordings by the Artist contained therein,
bears to the total number of recordings contained therein.

(d) One-half (1/2) of such respective preceding
amounts with respect to ninety percent (90%) of all
records manufactured, sold and paid for, and not returned, outside the limitations of the United States
of America. Royalties for records sold outside the
United States shall be computed in the national cur-
rency of the country where sold upon the wholesale
prices as herein stated in either the country of
manufacture or the country of sale, at Company's sole
option and are received by the Company in the United
States and in the dollar equivalent at the rate of
exchange at the time Company received payment.

(e) One-half (1/2) of such respective preceding
amounts with respect to ninety percent (90%) of all
tapes manufactured, sold and paid for, and not returned, outside the limitations of the United States

-2-

of America. Royalties for tapes sold outside the
United States shall be computed in the national cur-
rency of the country where sold upon the wholesale
prices as herein stated in either the country of
manufacture or the country of sale, at Company's sole
option and are received by the Company in the United
States and in the dollar equivalent at the rate of
exchange at the time Company received payment.

5. Notwithstanding anything to the contrary contained herein:

(a) in respect to phonograph records and/or tapes
sold and paid for, and not returned, through any Record
Club or by mail order or premium plan, the royalty payable to the Artist shall be one-half (1/2) the royalty
otherwise payable to the Artist with respect to such
phonograph records and/or tapes.

(b) no royalty shall be payable to the Artist with
respect to phonograph records and/or tapes which are
distributed to members of any Record Club either as a
result of joining such Club and/or as a result of the
purchase of a required number of records and/or tapes,
including records and/or tapes distributed as "bonus"
and/or "free" records and/or tapes.

(c) if the Artist's performances embodied on recordings released through any Record Club or by mail
order or premium plan shall not exceed fifty percent
(50%) of the total playing time of all performances
embodied on such recordings, the Artist shall not be
entitled to a royalty for such record and/or tape
providing Company is not paid.

6. Royalties on phonograph records included in albums,
jackets, boxes or any other style of package or container, such
as pre-recorded tape, shall be determined as if such records had
been sold separately and not so packaged.

7. The Company will compute such royalties within
sixty (60) days after June 30 and December 31 of each year during which records and/or tapes made hereunder are sold, for the
preceding six (6) month period, and will pay such royalties,
including any foreign royalties received and credited to the
Company's accounts, less any unrecorded advances or expenses
incurred by the Company under this agreement to the date of
such royalty statement.

8. All royalty statements and all other accounts then
rendered by the Company to the Artist shall be considered final
and absolute for the period covered and shall be binding upon
the Artist and not subject to any objection by the Artist for
any reason, unless specific objection in writing, stating the
basis thereof, is given to the Company within ninety (90) days
from the date of such statement.

All payments hereunder shall be to the order of
_____MARK LEVINE_____ And payments and
statements rendered to _MARK LEVINE_ at the
following address: _2409 McKINLEY AVE_
BERKELEY, CA 94703 shall be deemed rendered to and
received by the Artist hereunder.

9. All recordings hereunder and all derivatives made
therefrom, together with the performances embodied thereon, shall

be the sole and exclusive property of the Company. Without limiting the foregoing or any rights granted herein, but in addition thereto and without further payments, other than as herein provided the Artist grants to the Company:

(a) the right to manufacture, advertise, sell, lease, license or otherwise use or dispose of, in any or all fields of use throughout the world, or to refrain therefrom throughout the world or in any part thereof, records and/or tapes embodying the performances to be recorded hereunder, upon such terms and conditions as the Company may approve;

(b) the right to use and publish, and to permit others to use and publish, the Artist's name and likeness and all biographical material concerning the Artist: to write and publish, and to permit others to write and publish articles concerning the Artist for advertising or trade purposes in connection with the sale and exploitation of the Company's products, of Artist without limiting the generality of the foregoing, or otherwise, without restriction, and to use as descriptive of the Artist the phrase "Exclusive Catalyst Recording Artist", or "Exclusive Artist"; said words "Exclusive Artist" to be prefaced by any label or company name or names designated by the Company, or any other similar appropriate phrase, it being agreed that the Company may release or sell records and masters and/or tapes of selections made hereunder under its name and/or by any other name which, from time to time, may be selected by it;

(c) the sole and exclusive right in, title to and ownership of all masters, matrices, records and/or tapes or other reproductions of the performances embodied in such recordings by any method, electronic, magnetic, mechanical or other, now or hereafter known, obtained from recordings made hereunder and the performances embodied therein;

(d) the sole and exclusive right, if the Company so desires, to publicly perform the records and/or tapes and to permit public performances thereof, by means of radio broadcast or otherwise;

(e) the right to incorporate in records and/or tapes to be made hereunder instrumentations, orchestrations and arrangements owned by the Artist at the time of recording without payment therefor.

10. All arranged versions of musical compositions in the public domain composed by Artist alone or in conjunction with others, or arranged by them for recordings made hereunder shall be furnished to Company free of copyright-royalties. However, Company may, if it so elects, copyright any public domain arrangements, and any and all musical compositions written or controlled by the Artist.

11. The Artist hereby warrants and represents that he is under no disability, restriction or prohibition in respect to his right to execute this agreement and perform its terms and conditions hereunder.

12. The Company may, at its election, assign this agreement or any of its rights hereunder, to any person, major firm or corporation with national distribution; however, no assignment or transfer of this agreement shall be valid unless the assignee agrees to assume the Company's obligations hereunder.

13. This agreement shall be for a period of TWO (2) years from the date of execution hereof. The Artist hereby grants

-4-

to the Company the option to extend this agreement for_THREE__
(3) additional periods of one (1) year each under the same
terms and conditions hereof. Such options shall be considered
exercised by the Company unless the Company gives the Artist
notice to the contrary, in writing, at least thirty (30) days
prior to the expiration of the preceding term hereof. During
the initial contract period hereof, the Artist will perform
for the Company for the recording of a minimum of_TWENTY_(20)
satisfactory record sides, minimum of 5 minutes duration each.

14. The parties hereto specifically agree that, should
the Artist violate this agreement, all royalties due, or to become due, to the Artist shall be considered liquidated damages
and shall be forfeited by the Artist to the Company. For the
period in which a bona fide dispute exists between the Company
and the Artist, the Company shall report on, but not be required
to pay, royalties, providing any royalties payable are held in trust.

15. This agreement is subject to all rules and regulations of any union having jurisdiction. No failure of the Company
to perform because of such rules and regulations shall be deemed a
breach of this agreement.

16. For the purposes of this agreement, the following
definitions shall apply:

Recording Costs: All costs incurred in or incident to
the recording of the Artist's performance, including
but not limited to musicians', singers' and actors'
salaries and fees, fees payable to unions and to union
trust funds, cost of arrangements, copying charges,
cartage of musical instruments.

Record: Any device now or hereafter known, used for
the reproduction of sound by electrical, mechanical,
magnetic or other means.

Tape: Cassette, 4-track, 8-track, or reel-to-reel
sound reproductions embodying Artist's performances.

Video cassette, or any form of visual entertainment
using musical accompaniment.

17. This agreement shall be governed by the construed
under the laws of the State of California, U.S.A. It constitutes
the entire agreement between the parties and cannot be modified
except in writing, signed by both parties hereto. Invalidity or
unenforceability of any part of this agreement shall not affect
the validity or enforceability of the balance hereof.

18. Wherever in this agreement the singular form is
used, it shall be deemed to include the plural, and the masculine
gender shall include the feminine gender, wherever the context of
the agreement requires such substitution.

IN WITNESS WHEREOF, the parties hereto have executed
this agreement the day and year first above written.

By_____

Catalyst Records
A Division of Springboard Int'l

ARTIST:

Social Security No.

266-50-9051 .

-5-

APPENDIX B

*Royalty payments
to Mark Levine from
United Artists Records*

```
                    U A  RECORDS LTD
                    6 LANSING SQUARE STE 208
                    WILLOWDALE 425 ONT. CANADA

                CUARTERLY STATEMENT OF ROYALTIES
                                  FOR QUARTER ENDING
                                       09/30/74

    PUBLISHER - ETHIOPIA MUSIC                     ACCT. NO.
               C/O MR MARK LEVINE                  99-03860
               3810 SYCEUM AVE
               L A CALIF 90066

                                                  PAGE    1
    TITLE                    CATALOG NO   QTY    RATE    AMOUNT

    ****************************************************************

    THE CITY OF LA           BNLA 00260G   140   .020000    2.80
                                           SUBTOTAL         $2.80


                    TOTAL AMOUNT PAYABLE
                    EXCLUDING CR BAL SUBTOTALS        $2.80
```

6920 Sunset Boulevard, Los Angeles, California 90028
(213) 461-9141   Telex 67-3271   Cable UARECORDS

An Entertainment Service of
Transamerica Corporation

United Artists Records Inc

STATEMENT OF PUBLISHER ROYALTIES

		ACCOUNT NUMBER	PERIOD ENDING
ETHIOPIA MUSIC		001 - 05405	09-30-74
C/O THE HARRY FOX AGENCY, INC.			
110 E 59TH ST			
NEW YORK NY 10022			PAGE 1

CATALOG NUMBER	SELECTION	UNITS REPORTED	RATE	AMOUNT
	BALANCE DUE 06-30-74			.00
BNLA260G	CITY OF LA	999	.0200	19.98
		999 *		19.98
		999 **		19.98
	******** S U M M A R Y O F A C C O U N T ********			
	BALANCE-PRIOR STATEMENT		$	.00
	ADD-ROYALTIES EARNED-THIS PERIOD			19.98
	DEDUCT-CHARGES-THIS PERIOD			.00
	BALANCE-THIS STATEMENT		$	19.98

6920 Sunset Boulevard Los Angeles California 90028
[213] 461-9141 Telex 67 3271 Cable UARECORDS

An Entertainment Service of
Transamerica Corporation

United Artists Music and Records Group, Inc.

STATEMENT OF PUBLISHER ROYALTIES

ETHIOPIA MUSIC	**ACCOUNT NUMBER** 001 — 05405
C/O THE HARRY FOX AGENCY, INC.	
110 E 59TH ST	
NEW YORK NY 10022	

PERIOD ENDING 12-31-74

PAGE 1

CATALOG NUMBER	SELECTION	UNITS REPORTED	RATE	AMOUNT
	BALANCE DUE 09-30-74			19.98
BNLA260G	CITY OF LA	54	.0200	1.08
BNLA260G	CITY OF LA PX	15	.0200	.30
		69 *		1.38
	319512 111574 ROY P.F. 09-30-74			19.98-
		69 **		1.38
	******** S U M M A R Y O F A C C O U N T ********			
	BALANCE—PRIOR STATEMENT		$	19.98
	ADD—ROYALTIES EARNED—THIS PERIOD			1.38
	DEDUCT—CHARGES—THIS PERIOD			19.98-
	BALANCE—THIS STATEMENT		$	1.38

```
                        U A  RECORDS LTD
                        6 LANSING SQUARE STE 208
                        WILLOWDALE 425 ONT. CANADA

                   QUARTERLY STATEMENT OF ROYALTIES
                                        FOR QUARTER ENDING
                                             12/31/74

     PUBLISHER - ETHIOPIA MUSIC                    ACCT. NO.
              C/O MR MARK LEVINE                   99-03860
              3810 SYCRUM AVE
              L A CALIF 90066


                                                PAGE   1
     TITLE               CATALOG NO    QTY    RATE    AMOUNT

     **************************************************************

     THE CITY OF LA      BNLA 00260G    62  .020000      1.24
                                        SUBTOTAL         $1.24


                         TOTAL AMOUNT PAYABLE
                         EXCLUDING CR BAL SUBTOTALS       $1.24
```

6920 Sunset Boulevard Los Angeles California 90028
[213] 461-1141 Telex 67-3271 Cable UARECORDS

An Entertainment Service of
Transamerica Corporation

United Artists Music and Records Group, Inc.

STATEMENT OF PUBLISHER ROYALTIES

ETHIOPIA MUSIC	ACCOUNT NUMBER	PERIOD ENDING
C/O THE HARRY FOX AGENCY, INC.	001 - 05405	03-31-75
110 E 59TH ST		
NEW YORK NY 10022		PAGE 1

CATALOG NUMBER	SELECTION	UNITS REPORTED	RATE	AMOUNT
	BALANCE DUE 12-31-74			1.38
BNLA260G	CITY OF LA	311	.0200	6.22
BNEA260G	CITY OF LA	14-	.0200	.28-
ZNEA260G	CITY OF LA	96	.0200	1.92
		393 *		7.86
	217154 021475 RGY P.E. 12-31-74			1.38-
		393 **		7.86
	******** S U M M A R Y O F A C C O U N T ********			
	BALANCE-PRIOR STATEMENT		$	1.38
	ADD--ROYALTIES EARNED-THIS PERIOD			7.86
	DEDUCT-CHARGES-THIS PERIOD			1.38-
	BALANCE-THIS STATEMENT		$	7.86

6020 Sunset Boulevard Los Angeles California 90028
[213] 461-9141 Telex 67 32/1 Cable UARECORDS

An Entertainment Service of
Transamerica Corporation

United Artists Music and Records Group, Inc.

STATEMENT OF PUBLISHER ROYALTIES

ETHIOPIA MUSIC
C/O THE HARRY FOX AGENCY, INC.
110 E 55TH ST
NEW YORK NY 10022

ACCOUNT
NUMBER
001 - 05405

PERIOD
ENDING
06-30-75

PAGE 1

CATALOG NUMBER	SELECTION	UNITS REPORTED	RATE	AMOUNT
	BALANCE DUE 03-31-75			7.86
BNEA260G	CITY OF LA	2 -	.0200	.04
ZNEA260G	CITY OF LA	100	.0200	2.00
		98 *		1.96
	323437 051575 ROY P.E. 03-31-75			7.86-
		98 **		1.96

```
            ******** S U M M A R Y  O F  A C C C U N T ********
```

BALANCE-PRIOR STATEMENT		$ 7.86
ADD-ROYALTIES EARNED-THIS PERIOD		1.96
DEDUCT-CHARGES-THIS PERIOD		7.86-
BALANCE-THIS STATEMENT		$ 1.96

REPORT NO. RTN3-1

UNITED ARTISTS MUSIC & RECORD GROUP

NON SUBJECT PUBLISHER ROYALTIES

PERIOD ENDING 03 31 75

PUBLISHER	AGENT ACCOUNT	CATALOG	SELECTION	UNITS	RATE	AMOUNT
ETHIOPIA MUSIC	001 - 05405	BNL4260G	CITY OF LA	3,632	.0200	72.64
ETHIOPIA MUSIC	001 - 05405	BNE4260G	CITY OF LA	43	.0200	.85
			SONG TOTALS	3.675		72.50
			PUBLISHER TOTALS	3.675		73.50

110 EAST 59 STREET. NEW YORK, N.Y. 10022 • PLAZA 1-1950

Dial A rea Code 717
Cable Address HAFOX

June 16, 1978

To All Publishers:

We are enclosing herewith a statement and check representing royalties due you as the result of our examination of the books of United Artists Records for the period from January 1, 1973 to June 30, 1975.

This portion of the recovery consists of previously unpaid royalties due on the distribution of so-called "free" records in sales plans by United Artists Records.

Payments on account were made by United Artists Records pending a resolution of the claim. Interest accrued on these payments is being distributed to you per the attached check.

Very truly yours,

Albert Berman
President

AB:AMcG
Enc.

Index

Is Socialist Revolution in the U.S. Possible?

A Necessary Debate
MARY-ALICE WATERS
In two talks, presented as part of a wide-ranging debate at the Venezuela International Book Fairs in 2007 and 2008, Waters explains why a socialist revolution in the United States is possible. Why revolutionary struggles by working people are inevitable, forced upon us by the crisis-driven assaults of the propertied classes. As solidarity grows among a fighting vanguard of working people, the outlines of coming class battles can already be seen. $7. Also in Spanish and French.

Cuba and the Coming American Revolution

JACK BARNES
The Cuban Revolution of 1959 had a worldwide political impact, including on working people and youth in the imperialist heartland. As the mass, proletarian-based struggle for Black rights was already advancing in the U.S., the social transformation fought for and won by the Cuban toilers set an example that socialist revolution is not only necessary—it can be made and defended. This second edition, with a new foreword by Mary-Alice Waters, should be read alongside *Is Socialist Revolution in the U.S. Possible?* $10. Also in Spanish and French.

Revolutionary Continuity

Marxist Leadership in the U.S.
FARRELL DOBBS
How successive generations of fighters joined in the struggles that shaped the U.S. labor movement, seeking to build a class-conscious revolutionary leadership capable of advancing the interests of workers and small farmers and linking up with fellow toilers worldwide. 2 vols. *The Early Years: 1848–1917,* $20; *Birth of the Communist Movement: 1918–1922,* $19.

www.pathfinderpress.com

By Malcolm X

Malcolm X Talks to Young People
Four talks and an interview given to young people in Ghana, the United Kingdom, and the United States in the last months of Malcolm's life. This new edition contains the entire December 1964 presentation by Malcolm X at the Oxford University in the United Kingdom, in print for the first time anywhere. The collection concludes with two memorial tributes by a young socialist leader to this great revolutionary. $15. Also in Spanish.

Malcolm X Speaks
"Being here in America doesn't make you an American. No, I'm not an American. I'm one of the 22 million Black people who are the victims of Americanism. One of the 22 million Black people who are the victims of democracy, nothing but disguised hypocrisy." $20. Also in Spanish.

February 1965: The Final Speeches
Speeches from the last three weeks of the life of this outstanding leader of the oppressed Black nationality and of the working class in the United States. A large part is material previously unavailable, with some in print for the first time. $19

By Any Means Necessary
Speeches tracing the evolution of Malcolm X's views on political alliances, women's rights, intermarriage, capitalism and socialism, and more. $16

Malcolm X on Afro-American History
Recounts the hidden history of the labor of people of African origin and their achievements. $11

Also:
Two Speeches by Malcolm X, $5
Malcolm X: The Last Speeches, $17
Habla Malcolm X, $19

Order from www.pathfinderpress.com

Malcolm X, Black Liberation, and the Road to Workers Power
JACK BARNES

The foundations for the explosive rise of the Black liberation struggle in the U.S. beginning in the mid-1950s were laid by the massive migration of Blacks from the rural South to cities and factories across the continent, drawn by capital's insatiable need for labor power—and cannon fodder for its wars.

Malcolm X emerged from this rising struggle as its outstanding single leader. He insisted that colossal movement was part of a worldwide revolutionary battle for human rights. A clash "between those who want freedom, justice, and equality and those who want to continue the systems of exploitation."

Drawing lessons from a century and a half of struggle, this book helps us understand why it is the revolutionary conquest of power by the working class that will make possible the final battle for Black freedom—and open the way to a world based not on exploitation, violence, and racism, but human solidarity. A socialist world. $20. Also in Spanish and French.

The Working Class and the Transformation of Learning
The Fraud of Education Reform under Capitalism
JACK BARNES

"Until society is reorganized so that education is a human activity from the time we are very young until the time we die, there will be no education worthy of working, creating humanity." $3. Also in Spanish, French, Swedish, Icelandic, Farsi, and Greek.

The Communist Manifesto

KARL MARX AND FREDERICK ENGELS

Founding document of the modern working-class movement, published in 1848. Explains why communism is not a set of preconceived principles but the line of march of the working class toward power, "springing from an existing class struggle, a historical movement going on under our very eyes." $5. Also in Spanish, French, and Arabic.

Lenin's Final Fight

Speeches and Writings, 1922–23

V.I. LENIN

In the early 1920s Lenin waged a political battle in the leadership of the Communist Party of the USSR to maintain the course that had enabled the workers and peasants to overthrow the tsarist empire, carry out the first successful socialist revolution, and begin building a world communist movement. The issues posed in Lenin's political fight remain at the heart of world politics today. $20. Also in Spanish.

Capitalism and the Transformation of Africa

Reports from Equatorial Guinea

MARY-ALICE WATERS AND MARTÍN KOPPEL

An account of the transformation of production and class relations in this Central African country, as it is drawn deeper into the world market and both a capitalist class and modern proletariat are born. Here also the example of Cuba's socialist revolution comes alive in the collaboration of Cuban volunteer medical brigades helping to transform social conditions. Woven together, the outlines of a future to be fought for today can be seen—a future in which the toilers of Africa have more weight in world politics than ever before. $10. Also in Spanish.

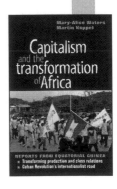

Capitalism's World Disorder
Working-Class Politics at the Millennium
JACK BARNES

The social devastation and financial panic, the coarsening of politics and politics of resentment, the cop brutality and acts of imperialist aggression accelerating around us—all are the product of lawful forces unleashed by capitalism. But the future the propertied classes have in store for us can be changed by the united struggle and selfless action of workers and farmers conscious of their power to transform the world. $25. Also in Spanish and French.

The Changing Face of U.S. Politics
Working-Class Politics and the Trade Unions
JACK BARNES

A handbook for the new generations coming into the factories, mines, and mills, as they react to the uncertain life, ceaseless turmoil, and brutality of capitalism. It shows how millions of working people, as political resistance grows, will revolutionize themselves, their unions and other organizations, and their conditions of life and work. $24. Also in Spanish, French, and Swedish.

The Jewish Question
A Marxist Interpretation
ABRAM LEON

Traces the historical rationalizations of anti-Semitism to the fact that Jews—in the centuries preceding the domination of industrial capitalism—were forced to become a "people-class" of merchants and moneylenders. Leon explains why the propertied rulers incite renewed Jew-hatred today. $20

Dynamics of the Cuban Revolution
A Marxist Appreciation
JOSEPH HANSEN

How did the Cuban Revolution unfold? Why does it represent an "unbearable challenge" to U.S. imperialism? What political obstacles has it overcome? Written as the revolution advanced from its earliest days. $25

www.pathfinderpress.com

Fighting Racism in World War II
From the pages of the **Militant**

A week-by-week account of the struggle against racism and racial discrimination in the United States from 1939 to 1945, taken from the pages of the socialist newsweekly, the *Militant*. $25

Socialism on Trial
JAMES P. CANNON

The basic ideas of socialism, explained in testimony during the trial of 18 leaders of the Minneapolis Teamsters union and the Socialist Workers Party framed up and imprisoned under the notorious Smith "Gag" Act during World War II. $16. Also in Spanish.

Thomas Sankara Speaks
The Burkina Faso Revolution, 1983–87

Colonialism and imperialist domination have left a legacy of hunger, illiteracy, and economic backwardness in Africa. In 1983 the peasants and workers of Burkina Faso established a popular revolutionary government and began to combat the causes of such devastation. Thomas Sankara, who led that struggle, explains the example set for Africa and the world. $24. Also in French.

Feminism and the Marxist Movement
MARY-ALICE WATERS

Since the founding of the modern revolutionary workers movement nearly 150 years ago, Marxists have championed the struggle for women's rights and explained the economic roots in class society of women's oppression. $5

How Far We Slaves Have Come!
South Africa and Cuba in Today's World

NELSON MANDELA AND FIDEL CASTRO

Speaking together in Cuba in 1991, Mandela and Castro discuss the unique relationship and example of the struggles of the South African and Cuban peoples. $10. Also in Spanish.

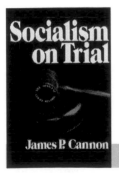  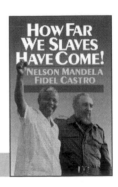

www.pathfinderpress.com

The Cuban Revolution and

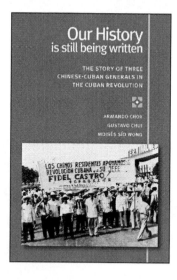

Our History Is Still Being Written
THE STORY OF THREE CHINESE-CUBAN GENERALS IN THE CUBAN REVOLUTION

In Cuba, the greatest measure against racial discrimination "was the revolution itself," says Gen. Moisés Sío Wong, "the triumph of a socialist revolution." Armando Choy, Gustavo Chui, and Sío Wong talk about the historic place of Chinese immigration to Cuba, as well as more than five decades of revolutionary action and internationalism, from Cuba to Angola and Venezuela today. Through their stories we see how millions of ordinary men and women changed the course of history, becoming different human beings in the process. $20. Also in Spanish and Chinese.

From the Escambray to the Congo
IN THE WHIRLWIND OF THE CUBAN REVOLUTION
Víctor Dreke

The author describes how easy it became after the Cuban Revolution to take down a rope segregating blacks from whites in the town square, yet how enormous was the battle to transform social relations underlying all the "ropes" inherited from capitalism and Yankee domination. Dreke, second in command of the internationalist column in the Congo led by Che Guevara in 1965, recounts the creative joy with which working people have defended their revolutionary course—from Cuba's Escambray mountains to Africa and beyond. $17. Also in Spanish.

Renewal or Death
Fidel Castro

"To really establish total equality takes more than declaring it in law," Fidel Castro told delegates to the 1986 congress of the Cuban Communist Party, pointing to the revolution's enormous conquests in the fight against anti-black racism. "We can't leave it to chance to correct historical injustices," he said. "We have to straighten out what history has twisted." In *New International* no. 6. $16

World Politics

The First and Second Declarations of Havana

Nowhere are the questions of revolutionary strategy that today confront men and women on the front lines of struggles in the Americas addressed with greater truthfulness and clarity than in these two documents, adopted by million-strong assemblies of the Cuban people in 1960 and 1962. These uncompromising indictments of imperialist plunder and "the exploitation of man by man" continue to stand as manifestos of revolutionary struggle by working people the world over. $10. Also in Spanish, French, and Arabic.

Che Guevara Talks to Young People

The Argentine-born revolutionary leader challenges youth of Cuba and the world to study, to work, to become disciplined. To join the front lines of struggles, small and large. To politicize themselves and the work of their organizations. To become a different kind of human being as they strive with working people of all lands to transform the world. Eight talks from 1959 to 1964. $15. Also in Spanish.

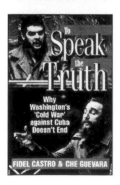

To Speak the Truth
WHY WASHINGTON'S 'COLD WAR' AGAINST CUBA DOESN'T END
Fidel Castro, Ernesto Che Guevara

In historic speeches before the United Nations General Assembly and other UN bodies, Guevara and Castro address the peoples of the world, explaining why the U.S. government fears the example of the socialist revolution in Cuba and why Washington's effort to destroy it will fail. $17

www.pathfinderpress.com

New International

A MAGAZINE OF MARXIST POLITICS AND THEORY

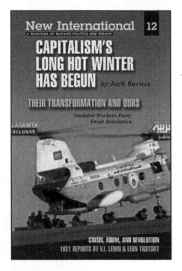

NEW INTERNATIONAL NO. 12

CAPITALISM'S LONG HOT WINTER HAS BEGUN

Jack Barnes

and "Their Transformation and Ours," **Resolution of the Socialist Workers Party**

Today's sharpening interimperialist conflicts are fueled both by the opening stages of what will be decades of economic, financial, and social convulsions and class battles, and by the most far-reaching shift in Washington's military policy and organization since the U.S. buildup toward World War II. Class-struggle-minded working people must face this historic turning point for imperialism, and draw satisfaction from being "in their face" as we chart a revolutionary course to confront it. $16

NEW INTERNATIONAL NO. 14

REVOLUTION, INTERNATIONALISM, AND SOCIALISM: THE LAST YEAR OF MALCOLM X

Jack Barnes

"To understand Malcolm's last year is to see how, in the imperialist epoch, revolutionary leadership of the highest political capacity, courage, and integrity converges with communism. That truth has even greater weight today as billions around the world, in city and countryside, from China to Brazil, are being hurled into the modern class struggle by the violent expansion of world capitalism."—Jack Barnes

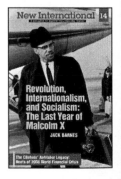

Also in No. 14: "The Clintons' Antilabor Legacy: Roots of the 2008 World Financial Crisis"; "The Stewardship of Nature Also Falls to the Working Class"; and "Setting the Record Straight on Fascism and World War II." $14

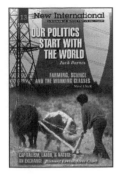

NEW INTERNATIONAL NO. 13

OUR POLITICS START WITH THE WORLD

Jack Barnes

The huge economic and cultural inequalities between imperialist and semicolonial countries, and among classes within almost every country, are produced, reproduced, and accentuated by the workings of capitalism. For vanguard workers to build parties able to lead a successful revolutionary struggle for power in our own countries, says Jack Barnes in the lead article, our activity must be guided by a strategy to close this gap.

Also: "Farming, Science, and the Working Classes" *by Steve Clark.* $14

NEW INTERNATIONAL NO. 11

U.S. IMPERIALISM HAS LOST THE COLD WAR

Jack Barnes

Contrary to imperialist expectations at the opening of the 1990s in the wake of the collapse of regimes across Eastern Europe and the USSR claiming to be communist, the workers and farmers there have not been crushed. The toilers remain an intractable obstacle to imperialism's advance, one the exploiters will have to confront in class battles and war. $16

NEW INTERNATIONAL NO. 8

CHE GUEVARA, CUBA, AND THE ROAD TO SOCIALISM

Articles by Ernesto Che Guevara, Carlos Rafael Rodríguez, Carlos Tablada, Mary-Alice Waters, Steve Clark, Jack Barnes

Exchanges from the opening years of the Cuban Revolution and today on the political perspectives defended by Guevara as he helped lead working people to advance the transformation of economic and social relations in Cuba. $10

NEW INTERNATIONAL NO. 5

THE COMING REVOLUTION IN SOUTH AFRICA

Jack Barnes

Writing a decade before the white supremacist regime fell, Barnes explores the social roots of apartheid in South African capitalism and tasks of urban and rural toilers in dismantling it, as they forge a communist leadership of the working class. $14

PATHFINDER AROUND THE WORLD

Visit our website for a complete list of titles and to place orders

www.pathfinderpress.com

PATHFINDER DISTRIBUTORS

UNITED STATES
(and Caribbean, Latin America, and East Asia)

*Pathfinder Books, 306 W. 37th St., 10th Floor,
New York, NY 10018*

CANADA

*Pathfinder Books, 7107 St. Denis, Suite 204,
Montreal, QC H2S 2S5*

UNITED KINGDOM
(and Europe, Africa, Middle East, and South Asia)

*Pathfinder Books, First Floor, 120 Bethnal Green Road
(entrance in Brick Lane), London E2 6DG*

SWEDEN

Pathfinder böcker, Bildhuggarvägen 17, S-121 44 Johanneshov

AUSTRALIA
(and Southeast Asia and the Pacific)

*Pathfinder, Level 1, 3/281-287 Beamish St., Campsie, NSW 2194
Postal address: P.O. Box 164, Campsie, NSW 2194*

NEW ZEALAND

*Pathfinder, 7 Mason Ave. (upstairs), Otahuhu, Auckland
Postal address: P.O. Box 3025, Auckland 1140*

Join the Pathfinder Readers Club
to get 15% discounts on all Pathfinder titles
and bigger discounts on special offers.
Sign up at www.pathfinderpress.com
or through the distributors above.